A Chinese Street Food Odyssey

A Chinese Street Food Odyssey

Helen and Lise Tse

Photography by Clare Winfield

PAVILION

CONTENTS

FOREWORD

I loved reading through *A Chinese Street Food Odyssey*. I felt like a fly on the wall as I travelled with my intrepid guides, Lisa and Helen Tse, throughout China. I was transported to many undiscovered, as well as familiar, dishes of the rich and varied street-food culture you can find there. Their experiences reverberate on every page as they describe in wonderful detail what could easily be a food diary. From my own experience as an author of cookery books, I was also impressed by the well-written and clear recipes. I know the authors want us to duplicate at home what they ate and enjoyed on the streets of China. The only missing part of this landmark book was the actual taste of the food... For that you need to get into your own kitchen and embark on a truly delicious voyage!

Ken Hom
BBC broadcaster and author

INTRODUCTION

To ensure we were giving you the most authentic and delicious versions of these recipes, Lisa and I did our research primarily by travelling to many parts of China and eating morning, noon and night. We have each gained 20kg (more than 40 pounds) doing the research for this book! We would taste the street food on offer and ask each other's opinion about the ingredients – some apparent and some less apparent. Some dishes were very familiar, others were totally new to us and for those, we'd ask the vendor whose version we felt was the tastiest to share their recipes with us. Many of those vendors were generous with their time and very patient, repeating the steps again and again so that we could capture the dish accurately in this book. Where it's difficult to replicate, we have given alternatives that come pretty close.

I write this book with my twin sister, Lisa, who is head chef at Sweet Mandarin, our restaurant in Manchester. I am the voice in the narratives, and Lisa has written and tested the recipes. Some of these recipes have been cooked for friends, family and even Premier Li Keqiang, the Prime Minister of China. He finished all the food on the plate and I was astounded when he asked for a private audience with the chefs – Lisa and me – to say thank you for the delicious food, 'the best Chinese food he had tasted in the UK'.

Our most vivid experience was walking through the street market of Beijing, where rows and rows of food stalls line the pedestrianized streets, with red lanterns glowing above. Smelling the mix of aromatic spices, caramelized apples, barbecuing meats and steaming dumplings made my stomach rumble and I wanted to try all the dishes. There are clouds of smoke as the cinders burn beneath the cooking meats and it's noisy – really noisy – with people jostling for the last bao (savoury bun), roasted meats, black chicken, sesame peanut brittle and hotpot of intestines. Piping hot bowls of noodles, coal-roasted squid, fried frogs' legs in soya milk and sweet potato shavings welcome the hungry, boisterous crowd. People are happy – and laughter makes the street food experience even tastier. I want to capture that sense of excitement, wonder and hunger for these morsels of street food.

Street food is accessible to all, but without being able to speak Chinese, the language barriers can make this feast rather one dimensional – more of an exercise in pointing. We want people to love Chinese food as much as we do, and to understand its diversity. There are eight main regional cuisines – Anhui, Cantonese (Guangdong), Fujian, Hunan, Jiangsu, Shandong (from which the Beijing style developed), Szechuan (Sichuan) and Zhejiang – but elements of each permeate through the culinary lineage and appear in the variety of street food recipes found throughout China. With this book we aim to open a window into China, to understand more fully each dish, its texture, colour, history and meaning, drawing on over 5000 years of civilization. Writing this book is our great challenge to bridge the gap between East and West. You only live once and we believe you should try things you have never tried before. Even if you never travel to China, we hope that our shared experiences will take you on an amazing culinary journey, where you will learn so much more than if you were just wandering around the street markets without an interpreter.

Best wishes
Lisa and Helen Tse MBE (Services to Food and Drink)

MEAT AND CHICKEN
肉和鸡

MAKES 8

PREP TIME
30 MINUTES,
PLUS 20 MINUTES
RISING

COOK TIME
20 MINUTES

PORK-FILLED BUNS

SHENGJIANBAO 生煎饅頭

A Shanghai speciality, *shengjianbao*, as they're known everywhere in China, are buns filled with juicy pork, then arranged in a flat, oil-slicked wok in which the bottoms are fried until they are crisp.

My uncle introduced me to *shengjianbao* at Shanghai's famous Dongxin Lu wet market; we both ran over to the street vendor. 'Hurry, they sell out fast,' called my uncle. Despite being in his seventies he was fit and still ran faster than me. I followed my nose. The smell was sensational – like salted caramel – as the bottoms of these buns were being fried. When I'd caught up with him, he'd already ordered a portion for each of us. I watched eagerly as they were fried in a huge cast-iron pan. I couldn't resist trying one there and then. Pillowy and light, enveloping minced pork with all its glorious juices, it was so tasty that I wanted to scoff the lot immediately.

We left the market with a bag of *shengjianbao* each and ran for the bus. It was time to say goodbye. I waved to my uncle as I clambered onto the bus and it immediately pulled away from the bus stop. Through the dusty windows, I caught the old man's eye, giving him a thumbs-up through the window. He was agitated and waving his hands and shouting, but I couldn't hear him. I thought – how sweet, he already missed my company. I waved back as the bus sped off.

It was only about 15 minutes into the journey, when the bus went off in a different direction, that I realized I was on the wrong bus. I shook my head in disbelief. That's what uncle had been trying to tell me. The bus rattled on, and I had no idea where I was going. Usually I'd be panic-stricken but I decided to just stay put and eat my *shengjianbao*. They were so tasty that I laughed off my mistake and enjoyed the scenic route. Being well fed with such delicious street food made me feel warm and happy. Dusk set in and the sunset glowed behind the narrow buildings. It is a beautiful memory and it made me realize there is a freedom associated with getting lost; I found this perfect travel moment, with a bag of these wonderful *shengjianbao*.

Dough

250g/9oz/2 cups plain (all-purpose) flour,
    plus extra for dusting

125ml/4fl oz/½ cup lukewarm water

½ tsp baking powder

1 tsp fast-acting dried yeast

1 tsp salt

1 tbsp caster (superfine) sugar

1 tsp sesame oil

Filling

300g/10½oz minced (ground) pork

100g/3½oz cabbage, finely chopped

5 spring onions (scallions), finely chopped

1 tsp salt

½ tsp ground white pepper

1 tbsp light soy sauce

1 tbsp potato starch

1 tsp sesame oil

Ingredients continue overleaf

To make the filling, put all the ingredients into a food processor and mix at high speed for 30 seconds. Transfer to a bowl and chill in the fridge for 30 minutes.

To make the dough, mix all the ingredients together in a large bowl until they form a smooth dough. Cover the bowl with clingfilm and leave in a warm place for 20 minutes until the dough has doubled in size.

Turn out the dough onto a lightly floured work surface and knead lightly until smooth. Roll it into a 32cm/13in log, then divide the log into eight equal pieces. Roll each piece into a ball, then flatten and use a rolling pin to roll out into 6cm/2½in diameter circles.

Wet your index finger with water and moisten the outer rim of a circle of dough. Place 2 heaped teaspoons of filling in the centre of the circle. If you are right-handed, hold the dough in the cupped palm of your left hand, or gently but firmly on a lightly floured worktop. Bring the dough up around the filling and pinch the edges together using the thumb and index finger of your right hand, working anticlockwise while turning the bun clockwise, creating little pleats all the way round. Close the top of the bun by twisting the pleated edge together and pinching to completely seal in the filling (see pictures on page 14). Reverse this if you are left-handed. Repeat to make eight buns. *Method continues overleaf.*

To cook

3 tbsp vegetable oil (see tips)

about 100ml/3½fl oz/
    scant ½ cup cold water

Dipping sauce

3 tbsp Chinese black vinegar

3 tbsp soy sauce

3 tbsp chilli oil

To cook the buns, heat a lidded frying pan – preferably non-stick – over a medium heat and add the oil. Place all the buns in the pan. It's OK if they stick together. Turn the heat to low and fry the buns for about 5 minutes until the base is golden brown and slightly crisp.

Pour the cold water into the pan, to a depth of about 1.5cm/⅝ inch, cover with a lid and cook for 10–15 minutes until all the water has evaporated. This will steam the buns and cook the filling.

To make the dipping sauce, mix the ingredients together in a small bowl. Serve the sauce with the hot buns.

Lisa's tips If your pan is not big enough, you may need to cook the buns in two batches to ensure they are fully cooked. Once the water has completely evaporated the buns should be ready to serve. Don't use too much oil to crisp the base, otherwise the dough will become very oily.

To fry the buns, use rapeseed (canola) oil, sunflower or groundnut (peanut) oil, but not olive oil, which has a low smoke point.

MAKES 8

PREP TIME
30 MINUTES,
PLUS 80 MINUTES
RISING AND RESTING

COOK TIME
20 MINUTES

PORK, LEEK AND CORIANDER BUNS

BAOZI 包子

We had just finished our tour around the *hutongs* (alleys) of Beijing when we saw a lady with a small cart selling these steaming buns. I asked her in Mandarin, 'What is that?' and she replied '*Zhūròu baozi*' – which means pork bun. When I bit into it, I loved how the coriander and leek complemented the pork in this traditional bun. Here is my version. *Illustrated overleaf.*

Dough

175ml/6fl oz/¾ cup lukewarm water

2 tsp fast-acting dried yeast

350g/12oz/scant 3 cups plain
  (all-purpose) flour, plus extra for dusting

2 tsp baking powder

50g/1¾oz/¼ cup caster (superfine) sugar

1 tsp salt

1 tbsp sesame oil

Filling

500g/1lb 2oz minced (ground) pork

3 leeks, finely chopped

5 sprigs of coriander (cilantro),
  finely chopped

5cm/2in piece of fresh root ginger,
  finely chopped

2 tbsp soy sauce

2 tbsp Shaoxing rice wine

1 tbsp caster (superfine) sugar

1 tsp Chinese five-spice powder

1 egg, beaten

1 tsp sesame oil

1 tsp potato starch

In a small bowl, mix the water with the yeast. Sift the flour and baking powder together into a large bowl and add the sugar and salt. Gradually add the yeast mixture and the sesame oil and mix until it forms a firm dough. Knead for 15 minutes until smooth. Put the dough in a bowl, cover with a damp tea towel and leave in a warm place for 1 hour until the dough has doubled in size.

Meanwhile, make the filling. Put all the ingredients in a large bowl and mix in a clockwise direction until the mixture is paste-like – do not put it in a food processor. Chill in the fridge for 15 minutes.

Turn out the dough onto a lightly floured work surface and knead lightly. Divide the dough into two equal parts; shape each part into a log and divide into four equal pieces. Roll out each piece into an 8cm/3in diameter circle, keeping the rolled-out dough covered with a damp tea towel.

Wet your index finger with water and moisten the outer rim of a circle of dough. Place 1 heaped tablespoon of filling in the centre of the circle. If you are right-handed, hold the dough in the cupped palm of your left hand, or gently but firmly on a lightly floured worktop. Bring the dough up around the filling and pinch the edges together using the thumb and index finger of your right hand, working anticlockwise while turning the bun clockwise, creating little pleats all the way round. Close the top of the bun by twisting the pleated edge together and pinching to completely seal in the filling (see pictures on page 14). Reverse this if you are left-handed. Repeat to make eight buns.

Line a large bamboo steamer with baking parchment (this will stop the buns from sticking). Place the completed *baozi* in the steamer and let them sit for 20 minutes before steaming: this will make the dough even more fluffy.

Place a trivet or round cake rack in a wok and fill the wok halfway with boiling water. Cover the steamer basket with its lid and place in the wok; steam over a high heat for 20 minutes. Serve hot.

MAKES 8

PREP TIME
1 HOUR,
PLUS 4 HOURS
MARINATING,
PLUS 50 MINUTES
RISING AND RESTING
COOK TIME
45 MINUTES FOR
THE CHAR SIU,
20 MINUTES STEAMING

STEAMED PORK BUNS

CHAR SHAO BAO 叉燒包

Hong Kong's old airport, Kai Tak, was a perilous descent among the skyscrapers and mountains. Even my dad, who is not religious, made the sign of the cross and said 'Thank God' when we landed safely. As soon as we exited the airport he led us across the road to the street vendor who made *char shao bao* and bought us all two each – one to eat now and one for later. As we waited for the vendor to bag the buns, we heard the noise. It was excruciatingly loud, as four aeroplanes flew out of Hong Kong towards the sea. The ground began to tremble, as did the multi-coloured umbrella which shaded the vendor's cart.

Dad wasn't too fussy when it came to eating on the street. Many locals ate en route as they were pressed for time. *Char shao bao,* also known as *char siu bao,* is a perfect snack and not messy to eat. Dad slotted right back into the Hong Kong lifestyle and picked up the pace of his walk, with suitcase in one hand and *bao* in the other; the rest of us fell into line like a row of ducklings following Papa duck to the hotel with our mum at the end. I remember slowly eating the white bun and saving the *char siu* centre until last. I was concentrating so much that I didn't see a taxi accelerate around the corner. I would have been flung into the air were it not for my dad using his suitcase to form a gate to fence me in and his full force to push me back. In the confusion of the moment, my half-eaten *bao* fell to the floor. My heart pounded. Dad's quick reaction was a shock to my system. I wasn't sure if my knees were trembling from fear or from losing half the *bao*! My bottom lip started to tremble … 'Don't cry. You need to look where you are going next time,' Dad scolded gently. He never let us eat *bao* on the street after that incident.

Usually these are filled with *char siu,* the sweet roasted pork recipe given here. Chicken can be substituted – in which case the buns would be called *ji ròu bao.* For the more adventurous, add salty braised pork belly with pickled cucumber for tang, hoisin sauce for sweetness and a squirt of sriracha hot chilli sauce and a sprinkling of crushed cashew nuts to keep things interesting. *Illustrated on previous page.*

Char siu

500g/1lb 2oz pork neck fillet

1 tsp Chinese five-spice powder

5 tbsp clear honey

2 tbsp tomato purée (paste)

3 tbsp hoisin sauce

5 tbsp light soy sauce

2 tbsp vegetable oil

Sauce

150ml/5floz/⅔ cup boiling water

2 tbsp clear honey

3 tbsp oyster sauce

2 tbsp light soy sauce

1 tbsp tomato purée

2cm/¾in piece of fresh root ginger, grated

To make the *char siu,* put the pork in a large bowl, sprinkle over the five-spice powder and rub it in well with your fingers. Combine 3 tablespoons of the honey with the tomato purée, hoisin sauce, soy sauce and oil in a separate bowl. Pour three-quarters of the mixture over the pork and rub into the meat. Cover the bowl of pork with clingfilm and set aside in the fridge to marinate for at least 4 hours. Cover the remaining marinade with clingfilm and set aside in the fridge, ready for basting the pork later.

To cook the pork, preheat the oven to 200°/400°F/gas 6. Line a roasting tin with foil, pour in 150ml/5floz/⅔ cup cold water and place a wire rack on top. Set the marinated pork on the rack and roast for 15 minutes. Remove the pork from the oven, baste all over with the reserved marinade and return to the oven for a further 15 minutes.

Remove the pork from the oven and baste all over with the remaining 2 tablespoons honey. Reduce the oven temperature to 180°C/350°F/gas 4 and return the pork to the oven for a further 15 minutes. Remove the roasted *char siu* from the oven and set aside to cool. Reduce the oven temperature to 110°C/225°F/gas ¼.

¼ tsp Chinese five-spice powder

1 tbsp caster (superfine) sugar

1 tbsp potato starch

1 tbsp Shaoxing rice wine

Dough

350g/12oz/scant 3 cups plain
   (all-purpose) flour, plus extra
   for dusting

2 tsp baking powder

2 tsp fast-acting dried yeast

50g/1¾oz/¼ cup caster (superfine) sugar

1 tsp salt

1 tbsp sesame oil

175ml/6fl oz/¾ cup lukewarm water

To make the sauce, combine all the ingredients in a saucepan and stir over a high heat for about 10 minutes until thick. Remove from the heat and set aside to cool.

Meanwhile, start making the dough. Sift the flour into a large bowl and stir in the baking powder, yeast, sugar, salt, sesame oil and water. Mix to form a dough and knead for 10 minutes until smooth. Cover the bowl with clingfilm and set aside in the cool oven for 30 minutes until the dough has doubled in size.

To finish the filling, cut half of the cold *char siu* into 1cm/½in dice and stir into the sauce. Keep the rest of the *char siu* in the fridge and use in dishes such as Soup-Filled Dumplings (see page 28), Rice Noodle Rolls (page 90) or Pork Puffs (page 24).

Turn out the dough onto a lightly floured work surface, cut into two equal pieces and roll into log shapes, approx. 30cm/12in long. Cut each log into four equal pieces, roll into balls and flatten with the palm of your hand. Using a rolling pin, roll out each piece into a 10cm/4in diameter circle.

Wet your index finger with water and moisten the outer rim of a circle of dough. Place 1 heaped tablespoon of filling in the centre of the circle. If you are right-handed, hold the dough in the cupped palm of your left hand, or gently but firmly on a lightly floured worktop. Bring the dough up around the filling and pinch the edges together using the thumb and index finger of your right hand, working anticlockwise while turning the bun clockwise, creating little pleats all the way round. Close the top of the bun by twisting the pleated edge together and pinching to completely seal in the filling (see pictures on page 14). Reverse this if you are left-handed. Repeat to make eight buns.

Line a large bamboo steamer with baking parchment (to stop the buns sticking). Arrange the buns in the steamer, leaving a 2cm/¾in gap between each bun to allow for expansion, and let them sit in the basket for 20 minutes before steaming: this will make the dough even more fluffy. Place a trivet or round cake rack in a wok and fill the wok with boiling water so it is just over a quarter full. Cover the steamer basket with its lid and place in the wok; steam over a high heat for 20 minutes. Turn off the heat and leave the lid of the steamer slightly ajar to allow some steam to escape for 2 minutes. Remove the buns from the steamer and serve hot.

Lisa's tip To get the buns very white you can use bleached flour, which can be found in Chinese supermarkets.

POT-STICKER DUMPLINGS

GUOTIE 鍋貼

MAKES 10

PREP TIME
40 MINUTES, PLUS
10 MINUTES RESTING
COOK TIME
ABOUT 10 MINUTES

Chinese New Year is a big celebration in China – shops, factories and schools shut for at least a week and families gather to enjoy home-cooked dishes such as guotie. *Guo tie* translates literally as 'pot stickers'. Like their thicker-skinned cousins *shengjianbao* (see page 12), they are first fried to create a crunchy base, then steamed to soften the dumpling skin and cook the meat. It never ceases to amaze me how beautiful these look once cooked. Soft and white on the top, with a golden brown, crisp bottom.

Dumpling wrappers

100ml/3½fl oz/7 tbsp boiling water

1 tsp salt

200g/7oz/generous 1½ cups strong white bread flour, plus extra for dusting

Filling

¼ head of Chinese leaf (napa cabbage), core removed, finely chopped

½ tsp salt

50g/1¾ oz chives, finely chopped

300g/10½oz minced (ground) pork

1 garlic clove, grated

5cm/2in piece of fresh root ginger, grated

1 tbsp Shaoxing rice wine

½ tbsp light soy sauce

1 tsp caster (superfine) sugar

½ tbsp oyster sauce

1 tsp sesame oil

2 tbsp potato starch or cornflour (corn starch)

To cook

1 tbsp vegetable oil

3 tbsp cold water

Dipping sauce

5 tbsp Chinese red vinegar

4–6 slices of fresh root ginger, cut into fine strips

First make the dumpling wrappers. Measure the boiling water into a jug, add the salt and stir to dissolve. Sift the flour two or three times into a large mixing bowl, pour in the salted water and mix with a wooden spoon to make a fairly stiff dough (you may need to add another 1–2 teaspoons boiling water). Turn out the dough onto a floured work surface and knead for 10 minutes until smooth, then return it to the bowl, cover with a clean tea towel and set aside at room temperature for 10 minutes.

Turn out the dough onto a lightly floured work surface, roll into a log and divide into 10 equal pieces. Shape each piece into a ball, then flatten and use a rolling pin to roll out into about 8cm/3in diameter circles. Arrange the dumpling wrappers in a stack on a plate, flouring in between each wrapper, cover with a clean tea towel and set aside while you make the filling.

To make the filling, put the cabbage in a large bowl and stir in the salt and chives. Squeeze the mixture between your hands to extract as much water as possible and drain well. Return the cabbage to the bowl and add the rest of the filling ingredients. Using a metal spoon, mix well in a clockwise direction until the filling is thoroughly combined and sticky in consistency.

Wet your finger with water and moisten the outer rim of a dumpling wrapper. Place 1 heaped tablespoon of filling in the centre of the circle, fold over to form a half-moon shape and pleat the edges together. If you are right-handed, do this from right to left. Use your left thumb to push the wrapper to your right and your right thumb and index finger to pinch the two layers of pastry together. Reverse this if you are left-handed. This creates a nice wavy edge. Repeat to make ten dumplings.

To cook, heat the oil in a large lidded frying pan over a medium heat. Place all the dumplings in the pan and fry them for 1 minute on each side until they have a golden crust. Pour in the cold water, immediately cover the pan with a lid and cook until the water has evaporated, about 5–6 minutes. Reduce the heat to low, then remove the lid and cook for a further minute.

For the sauce, mix the vinegar and ginger in a bowl and serve with the dumplings.

Lisa's tip Another way to cook these dumplings is to boil them first, for 5 minutes, then drain and pan-fry as above. This will ensure the meat is fully cooked in case you have been over-generous with the filling.

SHREDDED PORK WITH SWEET BEAN SAUCE

JING JIANG ROU SI 京酱肉丝

We grew up in a poor household, but that didn't stop my grandmother from telling us to dream big. If I wanted to eat lobster, she told me to close my eyes and imagine the next bite I was taking was lobster. That was a wonderful leap of imagination and I'll always be grateful for her teaching and discipline. So the story behind this dish touches my heart.

In the early 20th century, Lao Chen was a tofu maker in Beijing, selling the tofu and bean curd skins to neighbouring restaurants, including the famous Peking duck restaurants. His grandson would often ask his grandfather to buy him a duck – the smell of those roasted ducks was irresistible. But Mr Chen was too poor to buy a duck: the sale of tofu and tofu skins didn't earn much money. When Chinese New Year arrived he told his grandson he'd buy a duck; however, after counting all the pennies in his tin, he still didn't have enough. So Lao Chen bought pork, shredded it, mixed it with yellow bean sauce and told his grandson this was his version of the aromatic duck and pancakes. His grandson gobbled it up and really enjoyed it. When the grandson grew up, he could afford to buy duck and it struck him that it tasted quite different from the 'duck pancakes' his grandfather made him. The grandfather finally confessed that during that period of hardship he didn't want to crush the boy's dream of having duck for Chinese New Year so he had created his own version. The grandson was so overwhelmed by this story that he burst into tears and hugged his grandfather and thanked him for that protection and care. He continued to make this dish using pork out of respect for his grandfather.

200g/7oz pork fillet (tenderloin)

2–3 spring onions (scallions)

1 tbsp Shaoxing rice wine

1 tsp salt

1 egg, beaten

1 tbsp potato starch

vegetable oil for deep-frying

1 tbsp yellow bean paste
or yellow bean sauce

2 tsp sugar

1 tsp sesame oil

Chinese Crêpes (see page 126),
to serve

Slice the pork into matchstick-size strips. Slice the spring onions into matchstick strips and set aside.

Put the pork in a bowl, add the wine, salt, egg and potato starch and mix well.

Half-fill a wok or large saucepan with vegetable oil. Heat the oil to 180°C/350°F; if you don't have a cooking thermometer, test by dipping a wooden chopstick or wooden spoon into the oil – if bubbles immediately form around the chopstick the oil is hot enough. Using a slotted spoon, drop the pork into the oil and stir for 5–6 minutes until it is cooked and crispy. Drain on paper towels.

Pour off the oil into a metal container. Put 1 tablespoon of the oil back into the wok over a high heat. Add the yellow bean paste and fry for a minute or so, then add the sugar and sesame oil and 2–3 tbsp water to make a sauce. (If you are using yellow bean sauce, omit the water.)

Return the pork strips to the wok and toss well to coat the pork lightly in the sauce. Serve hot, with Chinese pancakes and the sliced spring onions, wrapping the pork in the pancake as you would with crispy aromatic Peking duck.

Lisa's tip If you are unable to find yellow bean paste, you can use hoisin sauce as an alternative.

BARBECUED PORK PUFFS

CHAR SHAO SU 叉燒酥

Probably one of the best ever variations of dim sum. Crisp puff pastry wraps a filling of savoury yet sweet Cantonese barbecued pork, and the edges of the pastry are encrusted with the oozy sauce. The *char shao*, or *char siu,* puffs are probably even more delicious cold than hot, as the filling almost melts into the pastry and the flavour of the pork intensifies once it cools. If you have leftover *char siu* from making Steamed Pork Buns (see page 18), you can use it to fill these puffs.

500g/1lb 2oz ready-made puff pastry

flour for dusting

1 egg, beaten

1½ tbsp sesame seeds

Quick char siu

2 tbsp vegetable oil,
  plus extra for greasing

1 small onion, diced

100g/3½oz cooked pork,
  cut into small cubes

1 tbsp honey

1 tbsp dark soy sauce

1 tbsp soft brown sugar

¼ tsp Chinese five-spice powder

2 tbsp water

½ tsp sesame oil

1 tsp potato starch

To make the *char siu*, heat a frying pan or wok over a high heat, add the vegetable oil and when it is hot add the onion and cook for about 3 minutes until softened. Add the remaining ingredients, except the potato starch. Cook for a further 5 minutes. Then add the potato starch to slightly thicken the filling. Transfer to a bowl and set aside to cool.

Preheat the oven to 200°C/400°F/gas 6. Grease a baking sheet.

Lightly dust a work surface with flour and roll out the pastry as thinly as possible, about 2–3mm/⅛in thick. Cut out eight 10cm/4in squares. Add 1 tablespoon of the filling to each square. Brush the edges with beaten egg and fold over to make triangles, pressing the edges to seal. Brush the tops of the parcels with beaten egg and sprinkle with sesame seeds.

Place the pastries on the baking sheet and bake for about 15 minutes until golden brown.

Lisa's tip Make sure the filling is cool before you use it; if it is still warm the steam may make the pastry parcel break or become soggy.

PORK CHOP BUN

ZHU PA BAO 豬扒包

A pork chop bun, known as a Macanese hamburger, is one of the most popular snacks in Macao. Macao is a small peninsula in mainland China, across the Pearl River Delta from Hong Kong, and it was a Portuguese overseas territory until 1999. When I visited recently, it reflected a mix of Portuguese and Chinese influences. Famous for its giant casinos and extravagant malls, Macao has earned the nickname, the 'Las Vegas of Asia'. As I walked to one of its more striking landmarks, the 338m/1110ft-high Macau Tower, with sweeping city views, I tried a pork chop bun. There is something seriously sweet and fresh about this snack, and the pork chop has more bite than a burger; it's served plain – no lettuce or tomato. These are perfect to enjoy towards the end of a night out, especially after a flutter at the casinos where you may have lost your shirt!

400g/14oz boneless pork cutlets/chops

1 tsp Chinese five-spice powder

1 tsp salt

1 tbsp sesame oil

1 tbsp soy sauce

2 tbsp vegetable oil

4 brioche buns, to serve

Marinate the pork cutlets with the five-spice powder, salt, sesame oil and soy sauce for at least 15 minutes – or preferably overnight.

Heat a frying pan over a medium–high heat and when hot add the vegetable oil. Fry the pork cutlets for about 3 minutes on each side until the pork is cooked through (the meat will be very firm to the touch).

Slice open the buns and add the pork cutlets. Street food at its simplest.

Lisa's tip If you don't like pork, try this with sirloin steak – delicious.

SERVES 4 (MAKES
ABOUT 12)

PREP TIME
20 MINUTES, PLUS
10 MINUTES CHILLING
COOK TIME
20 MINUTES

THREE OF A KIND

JIAN NANG SAN BAO 煎釀三寶

This is a traditional street food that can be found on most street vendors' stalls in Guangdong, Hong Kong and Macao, especially in the busy shopping districts, attracting hungry shoppers and people succumbing to a snack on their way home from work. Three of a kind usually includes aubergine, peppers and tofu, filled with a minced prawn mixture, pierced with a bamboo stick for ease of eating on the go, to be dipped in a sauce such as soy sauce, chilli sauce or oyster sauce. Vendors have now expanded their offering to include stuffed mushrooms, bitter melon and sausage. I always try to buy the biggest pieces possible and ensure they are charred to bring out the sweetness of the aubergine, pepper or mushroom.

1 aubergine (eggplant)

1 green pepper, deseeded and cut
into quarters

4 large button mushrooms

2 eggs, beaten

3 tbsp potato starch

vegetable oil for deep-frying

Filling

200g/7oz raw peeled king prawns
(shrimp), deveined

300g/10½oz minced (ground) pork

2 egg whites

2 tbsp Shaoxing rice wine

1 tsp salt

1 tsp caster (superfine) sugar

¼ tsp ground white pepper

1 tbsp sesame oil

To make the filling, combine the prawns, pork, egg whites, wine, salt, sugar and pepper in a food processor and blitz to a smooth paste. Add the sesame oil and blitz briefly to combine.

Cut the aubergine into four thick slices (about 4–5cm/1½–2in lengths) and scoop out some of the flesh. Press 1½ teaspoons of the filling inside each piece of aubergine. Dip into the beaten egg and then into the potato starch to coat. This will help the filling to stay in place.

Put 1½ teaspoons of the filling onto each piece of green pepper, press down gently, then coat in beaten egg and potato starch as for the aubergine.

Pull the stalks out of the mushrooms, leaving a hollow centre. Put 1½ teaspoons of the filling into each mushroom, then coat in beaten egg and potato starch.

Put all the filled vegetables into the fridge for 10 minutes to firm up.

Half-fill a wok or saucepan with vegetable oil. Heat the oil to 180°C/350°F; if you don't have a cooking thermometer, test by dipping a wooden chopstick or wooden spoon into the oil – if bubbles immediately form around the chopstick, the oil is hot enough. If it is not, it will make this dish soggy. Put the filled aubergine, green pepper and mushrooms into the hot oil and use a slotted spatula or spider to hold the pieces under the oil. Cook for 5–8 minutes until the filling is cooked and firm to the touch. (Cook in batches to prevent the oil from dropping in temperature.) Drain on paper towels and serve with soy sauce or oyster sauce.

Lisa's tip If you have any filling left over it can be shaped into balls and deep-fried, to enjoy along with the filled vegetables.

MAKES 12

PREP TIME
1½ HOURS, PLUS
2 HOURS FREEZING
COOK TIME
10 MINUTES, PLUS
45 MINUTES FOR
THE STOCK

SOUP-FILLED DUMPLINGS

XIAOLONGBAO 小籠包

In China, people don't queue. I can't tell you the number of times I have been queue-jumped and how infuriated I was. However, if you want to eat *xiaolongbao* in Nanxiang, a suburb of Shanghai in the Jiading District, you queue. This is where *xiaolongbao* were invented about 100 years ago, and they are still sold here, near Nanxiang's notable park, Guyi Garden. When I went there, the queue went around the block and no one queue-jumped because that would result in an immediate ban from the stall and no dumplings.

Xiaolongbao are now found throughout Shanghai and beyond. They are traditionally filled with pork, sometimes with the addition of crab or prawns; more modern innovations include other meats, seafood and vegetarian fillings. The characteristic soup-filled kind are created by wrapping some savoury meat jelly inside the skin alongside the meat filling. As the buns steam, the jelly melts into soup.

When I bit into these delicious dumplings, the soup inside burst out and slightly burned my tongue. That was me being too hasty. I absolutely love these dumplings and would have queued again for another portion, but I've learnt in China to always save room for dessert!

Chicken stock

300g/10½oz chicken wings

150g/5½oz pork loin or spare ribs

1 knob of fresh root ginger

4 garlic cloves

3 spring onions (scallions),
   roughly chopped

500ml/17fl oz/2 cups water

2 tbsp powdered gelatine

Filling

350g/12oz minced (ground) pork

1 tsp Shaoxing rice wine

2–3 spring onions (scallions),
   finely chopped

1 tsp salt

1 tsp sugar

1 tsp sesame oil

Wrappers

350g/12 oz/scant 3 cups plain
   (all-purpose) flour, plus extra for dusting

1 tsp salt

100ml/3½fl oz/scant ½ cup boiling water

3 tbsp ice-cold water

Dipping sauce

5 tbsp Chinese red vinegar

4–6 slices of fresh root ginger,
   cut into fine strips

To make the stock, put all the ingredients except the gelatine into a stock pot and bring to the boil. Reduce the heat and simmer for 20 minutes. Skim off any froth. Strain the broth into a bowl and skim off any fat from the surface. Pour back into the cleaned pan and boil to reduce by half, which will take about 10 minutes. Set aside 100ml/3½fl oz/scant ½ cup of the stock to make the filling.

Sprinkle the gelatine over a little cold water and leave to soak for 5 minutes. Add the gelatine to the reduced stock and mix well. Pour into a shallow container and leave to cool, then transfer to the freezer for 2 hours. When frozen, cut into small cubes, about 2cm/¾in, and transfer to the fridge.

To make the filling, put all the ingredients into a bowl together with the reserved stock and mix thoroughly for 1 minute. Cover the bowl with clingfilm and put in the fridge for up to 2 hours until the filling has firmed up.

To make the wrappers, put the flour and salt into a bowl and add the boiling water, stir to combine, then add the cold water. Knead for 10 minutes until smooth. Shape the dough into a long log and divide into 12 equal pieces. Shape each piece into a ball, then flatten with the palm of your hand and roll out to a 7–8cm/3in circle, using a rolling pin. Repeat to make 12 wrappers.

Moisten the outer rim of a wrapper. Place 1 heaped tablespoon of filling in the centre of the circle and add a cube of jellied stock. If you are right-handed, hold the dough in the cupped palm of your left hand, or rest on a lightly floured worktop. Bring the dough up around the filling and pinch the edges together using the thumb and index finger of your right hand, working anticlockwise while turning the bun clockwise, creating little pleats all the way round. The traditional *xiaolongbao* has 24 pleats but you can make fewer. Close the top of the bun by twisting the pleated edge together and pinching to completely seal in the filling (see pictures on page 14). Reverse this if you are left-handed. Repeat to make 12 dumplings. Grease 12 disposable foil cupcake cases with a smudge of oil and put a dumpling in each.

To cook the dumplings, fill a wok with boiling water so it is just over a quarter full. Place the dumplings in a large bamboo steamer basket. Cover the steamer basket with its lid and place in the wok; steam for 10 minutes over a high heat.

For the dipping sauce, mix the vinegar and ginger in a small bowl. Serve the dumplings with the sauce.

Lisa's tip It's worth buying disposable foil cupcake cases to cook and serve the dumplings, and to prevent the hot liquid from spilling out.

SERVES 4
(MAKES 12)

PREP TIME
20 MINUTES
COOK TIME
10 MINUTES

STEAMED PORK AND PRAWN DUMPLINGS

SHAO MAI 燒賣

Shao Mai, or *siu mai*, were first served in a tea house along the Silk Road during the Ming dynasty. The pork and prawn filling sits in a little cup made of a thin wonton wrapper.

12 wonton wrappers

12 peas

Filling

100g/3½oz pork loin, cut into small dice

175g/6oz raw peeled king prawns (shrimp), deveined and cut into small dice

1 spring onion (scallion), finely sliced

3 dried Chinese mushrooms, soaked in hot water for 20 minutes, then finely sliced

1 tsp salt

1 tsp sugar

1 tbsp water

pinch of ground white pepper

1 tbsp Shaoxing rice wine

1 tbsp sesame oil

1 tbsp light soy sauce

2 tsp potato starch

To make the filling, put all the ingredients into a bowl and mix together using your hand (wear disposable gloves if you don't like touching raw meat or prawns); gather the mixture together and slam it down into the bowl until it comes together (this breaks down the protein and softens it); do not put the mixture into a food processor as you do not want it too smooth. Cover the bowl with clingfilm and leave the filling in the fridge for about 10 minutes to firm up.

Trim the corners of the wonton wrappers to make them round rather than square.

To make the dumplings, cup the fingers of your left hand and place a wonton wrapper in your cupped fingers. Place 1 tablespoon of filling in the centre of the wrapper. Using your fingers, squeeze the filling into the pastry so it becomes a little cup. Using a butter knife, gently flatten the filling, then place a pea in the centre. Place the dumplings in a greased bamboo steamer basket or on a greased heatproof plate.

To cook the dumplings, place a trivet or round cake rack in a wok and add boiling water so that it is just over a quarter full. Put the steamer basket or plate on top of the trivet, cover with a lid and steam the dumplings for 7–8 minutes. You can check that they are cooked by pressing a dumpling with your finger; it will feel firm to the touch. If the meat still looks raw then cook for a further minute or so. Serve immediately.

Lisa's tips *Shao mai* can be frozen raw and cooked from frozen. The steaming time will be approximately 25–30 minutes.

You can fill these with any filling you want, such as chicken, prawn, crab or beef.

TAIWANESE PANCAKE

TAI WAN SHOU ZHUA BING 台湾手抓饼

Although this pancake originated from Taiwan, its popularity in Shanghai and at other street markets around China has made it a Chinese bestseller. The pancake is generally savoury with various toppings such as pork floss (a very light dried meat product, sold in Asian supermarkets, sometimes under the name *rouxuong*, or *rousong*), a fried egg, hot dog, tomatoes or lettuce, along with a drizzle of sweet and sour sauce. What I love about this is that it's easy to eat and every bite has different ingredients. No matter where you are in the world, wraps are a popular street food offering.

Pancakes

100g/3½oz/generous ¾ cup plain (all-purpose) flour

250ml/9fl oz/1 cup cold water

1 tsp salt

3 tbsp vegetable oil for frying

Filling

4 eggs

4 canned frankfurters

½ iceberg lettuce, sliced

1 tomato, sliced

4 tbsp pork floss (*rouxuong*, or shredded cooked pork loin)

sriracha hot chilli sauce, or any sauce of your choice

To make the pancakes, mix the flour, water and salt in a bowl to make a smooth batter. Heat a frying pan over a high heat, add the vegetable oil and then pour a ladle of the batter into the frying pan, making it as thin as possible. Cook for 1–2 minutes until golden brown, then toss the pancake to cook the other side. Transfer to a warmed plate and make three more pancakes in the same way.

Using the same frying pan, crack the eggs and fry them the way you like them. Reheat the frankfurters for 3–4 minutes.

Fill each pancake with a fried egg, a frankfurter, lettuce, tomato and a tablespoon of pork floss. Add the sauce, roll up the pancake and enjoy.

Lisa's tip If you are worried about the pancake fillings falling out of the bottom, use foil to make a pocket for the pancake so you can eat on the go.

SERVES 4–6

PREP TIME
10 MINUTES,
PLUS MAKING THE
FLATBREADS
COOK TIME
10 MINUTES

CHINESE BURGERS

ROU JIA MO 肉夹馍

These sandwiches are sometimes called Chinese hamburgers. The flatbread recipe is the same as that used with the Mutton Stew (see page 40). The filling is generally pork, but you could substitute chicken or beef or even tofu. The meat is flavoured with spring onions and chillies, really lifting this street-food classic.

I remember seeing the tiniest kitchen on the corner of a street in Shenzhen – it could have been a toy kitchen. I watched a husband and wife team knead, roll and cook the flatbreads on one little hob before using the same pan to fry off the pork filling. They even had a makeshift sign 'BURGER', which was comical as their stand was right opposite McDonald's. That's the entrepreneurial spirit of China. After all, a burger is just two pieces of bread around a meat filling. I could smell the wonderful savoury filling a street away and it enticed me to buy one. Call it what you like, this was indeed a 'burger' to be reckoned with. The woman laughed and asked me, had I not eaten for decades? I just stood there and scoffed the lot – that's how good it was. The next day I returned and hovered as they made their wares; I bought two. On the third day they taught me how to make this dish, which I am delighted to share with you. Thank you indeed to Mr and Mrs Wang for your amazing recipe for what is arguably one of the best burgers I have ever eaten.

4–6 Flatbreads (see page 40)

4 tbsp vegetable oil

1 large onion, finely sliced

3 garlic cloves, finely chopped

300g/10½oz minced (ground) pork,
   or slices of pork about 5mm/¼in thick

150ml/5fl oz/⅔ cup chicken stock

1 whole star anise

2 bay leaves

1 piece of orange peel

½ tsp chilli powder

1 fresh red chilli, finely sliced (optional)

1 tbsp sesame oil

3 spring onions (scallions), finely sliced

First make the flatbreads, cook them and set aside.

Heat a large frying pan or wok over a high heat, add the vegetable oil and fry the onion and garlic for 3 minutes until the onion has softened. Add the pork and stir-fry until browned, then add the stock, star anise, bay leaves and orange peel and cook for 5 minutes or until the pork is fully cooked.

Add the chilli powder, red chilli, if using, and sesame oil, stir to combine, then turn off the heat. Discard the star anise, bay leaves and orange peel. Add the spring onions and stir to combine – you want to keep their freshness and crunch.

Slice a flatbread in half, and add a heaped tablespoon of the filling. Take a bite and you're in street food heaven.

Lisa's tip You could use pork belly, diced into small pieces, instead of the minced pork.

SERVES 4

PREP TIME
10 MINUTES,
PLUS 20 MINUTES
MARINATING
COOK TIME
10 MINUTES, OR
25 MINUTES ON
THE BONE

SPARE RIBS

PAI GU 排骨

Spare ribs are an inexpensive cut of pork (or beef) and their versatility – fried, steamed or braised – makes them a favourite ingredient of the Chinese. In this recipe they are steamed with salty black beans. The recipe works equally well whether you use boneless meat or spare ribs on the bone.

If Dad's at home he's always in the kitchen. It's his favourite place. We've always spent a lot of time there, cooking, eating and talking. Everything in our family revolves around food. Dad works very long hours, slogging hard at the woks, often hidden in billowing smoke, but these spare ribs are an easy dish because once they're being steamed he's hands free. With this dish, he's relaxed, and it reminds me of those good times with my dad.

250g/9oz boneless pork spare rib meat, or
   750g/1lb 10oz spare ribs on the bone

2 tbsp vegetable oil

2 garlic cloves, chopped

2 spring onions (scallions), chopped

2 tbsp fermented (salted) black beans,
   gently crushed

1 small red chilli, chopped

Marinade

2 tbsp oyster sauce

1 tbsp Shaoxing rice wine

1 tbsp light soy sauce

½ tbsp dark soy sauce

½ tbsp sugar

½ tsp salt

1 tbsp potato starch

3 tbsp water

2 tsp vegetable oil

Chop the spare ribs into small pieces, approx. 2cm/¾in wide. When chopping ribs on the bone it's best to place a damp tea towel under the chopping board to prevent it from sliding on the work surface.

Heat a wok over a medium–high heat, add 1 tablespoon of the oil and fry the garlic, spring onions, black beans and chilli for 5 minutes.

Mix together all the marinade ingredients in a bowl, add the chopped ribs and mix well to coat with the marinade. Add the black bean mixture and stir to combine. Leave in the fridge to marinate for 20 minutes.

Place the pieces of meat with the garlic, chilli and black beans on a plate and place the plate in a bamboo steamer basket. Place a trivet or round cake rack in a wok, and add boiling water so that it is just over a quarter full. Put the steamer basket on top of the trivet, cover with a lid and steam over a high heat for 10 minutes, or 25 minutes if the meat is on the bone.

Lisa's tip If you can't find fermented black beans you can substitute a jar of black bean sauce, which will give the same aromatic and smoky flavour.

BEIJING SAUSAGE

BEI JING CHANG 北京腸

MAKES 4

PREP TIME
30 MINUTES
COOK TIME
10 MINUTES

'Please could I have a sausage?' asked my sister.

I burst into laughter. 'You mean they make sausages in China?'

'They do! Look over there!'

I turned and saw a vendor with a red and white striped cart selling what looked like jumbo hot dog sausages. I shook my head in disbelief. I went over to the vendor and asked her to explain whether these sausages were actually of Chinese origin or just for the American tourists?

She replied quite vehemently that I had better brush up on my Chinese history before accusing her of making American sausages. She was extremely proud of her sausages, and said the recipe originated from the Ming dynasty.

I asked her what was so different about these Chinese sausages. 'Have a bite,' she said. I bit into one and it was so spicy. I stuck my tongue out, gasping for a drink. After the numbing had subsided and the sausage had cooled down slightly I took another bite. As well as the chilli I tasted a hint of five-spice. I had learnt something new today and my sister couldn't stop laughing at me. I had turned red – partly from embarrassment at being lambasted by this sausage lady and partly from the chillies.

To make sausages you will need a mincer with a sausage filler attachment; if you have one you'll be able to make sausages from all kinds of meats and flavourings. You'll also need to buy some sausage casing from the butcher; when buying, check whether it needs to be soaked for a few hours before you fill it.

250g/9oz minced (ground) pork

2 garlic cloves, finely chopped

50g/1¾oz onion, finely chopped

50g/1¾oz chives, chopped

½ tsp Chinese five-spice powder

3 tbsp water

about 70cm/28in sausage casing,
 soaked if necessary

hot chilli sauce (optional), to serve

Poaching broth

200ml/7fl oz/generous ¾ cup chicken stock

2 tsp chilli bean paste

½ tsp salt

1 tsp sugar

1 tsp sesame oil

3 spring onions (scallions)

2cm/¾in piece of fresh root ginger, sliced

In a bowl, mix the pork, garlic, onion, chives, five-spice and water until the mixture is paste-like. Fill the mixture into the sausage casing to make four 10cm/4in long sausages.

Put the stock into a saucepan and add the chilli bean paste, salt, sugar, sesame oil, spring onions and ginger. Bring to the boil, then turn off the heat. Add the sausages, cover and leave for 10 minutes.

Remove the sausages from the broth. Heat a griddle pan or frying pan over a high heat and sear the sausages on both sides for 2–3 minutes. Serve as they are or with a hot chilli sauce.

DAN DAN NOODLES

DAN DAN MIAN 担担面

Dan dan in Chinese is the sound made when a stick beats something hard. The thing being beaten here is the dough for the noodles. In Sichuan, I watched the chef mix the flour and water into a sticky dough, which was then beaten on a floury surface until it formed a long strip; the strip was folded and beaten again and again. Finally the dough was whirled like a skipping rope, pulling and folding it to make long thin white noodles that were hung over a wooden pole to prevent them from sticking. The pole was used to transport them to the streets where they were sold to passers-by. The sauce typically used in this dish is hot and spicy; the noodles soak up the flavours like a sponge and there is spice, heat and intensity in every bite.

3 tbsp vegetable oil

300g/10½oz minced pork

2 tbsp soy sauce

1 tbsp Shaoxing rice wine

1 tsp Chinese five-spice powder

1 tsp finely chopped garlic

100g/3½oz *ya cai* (preserved mustard greens) or pickled gherkins, finely chopped

250g/9oz fresh Chinese noodles or udon noodles

2–3 spring onions (scallions), finely chopped, to garnish

Dan dan sauce

2 tsp Chinese sesame paste

1 tsp finely chopped garlic

4 tbsp soy sauce

1 tsp ground Sichuan peppercorns

1 tsp sugar

3 tbsp chilli oil

1 tsp sesame oil

2 tbsp Chinese black vinegar

200ml/7fl oz/generous ¾ cup chicken stock

Heat a wok over a high heat. Add the vegetable oil and, when smoking, add the minced pork and stir-fry for 4–5 minutes until cooked. Add the soy sauce, wine, five-spice powder, garlic and *ya cai* and stir well. Set aside.

For the sauce, put all the ingredients in a bowl and mix until smooth. Set aside.

Cook the noodles in boiling water for 4–5 minutes. Drain and rinse the noodles in cold water. Drain well, then add the noodles to the bowl with the sauce. Mix well.

Divide the noodles between two serving bowls and spoon a generous amount of the minced pork mixture on top. Serve at once, sprinkled with spring onions.

LAMB SKEWERS

YÁNGRÒU CHUAN 羊肉串

MAKES 8

PREP TIME
15 MINUTES, PLUS
AT LEAST 30 MINUTES
MARINATING
COOK TIME
10–15 MINUTES

Xinjiang, a vast region in western China, is predominantly Muslim. One of the best-known street foods from this region is *yangrou*, or lamb skewers. The vendors wear long tunics and skull caps and their features look more Indian than Chinese; the Indian influence is also reflected in the cooking method, as these skewers are cooked in a tandoor, a cylindrical oven made of clay or metal.

At the foot of the mountains was a stall where a tall man stood, looking like the boss. It felt like it was six in the morning, but it was actually closer to noon. There were a few punters, mostly elderly, lazily resting on the tables, but no one was serving them. The walls of the room were unpainted breeze blocks and the counter was greasy to touch. To be honest it didn't look very appetizing or welcoming but our tour guide insisted we get the *yangrou* here at this small café.

'You asked me to bring you to a place where the locals eat *yangrou*. Here it is. It's not fancy but the food is good.'

We sat and waited for about 25 minutes for the *yangrou* to be cooked and we watched the place come alive with customers. By the time our dishes were ready the place was full and a queue was forming at the door.

The lamb was very juicy and tender, its texture meltingly soft. A piece of lamb fat that had been skewered between two chunks of meat had melted slightly, adding a deeper flavour to the skewered lamb, and I appreciated how clever that simple technique was in helping to soften the meat as well as giving the dish its unique flavour. You don't need a tandoor to make this recipe; a griddle pan works very well.

400g/14oz shoulder of lamb,
  cut into bite-sized pieces

2 lemons, cut into wedges,
  to serve

Marinade

4 tbsp vegetable oil

3 tsp dried chilli flakes

1 tbsp ground cumin

1 tsp ground nutmeg

1 tsp ground ginger

1 tsp ground coriander

3 garlic cloves, finely
  chopped

1½ tsp salt

3 tbsp light soy sauce

Soak 8 wooden skewers in water for 30 minutes.

Combine the ingredients for the marinade in a small bowl. Pour two-thirds of the marinade over the lamb, cover and refrigerate for 30 minutes so the marinade can flavour and tenderize the lamb.

Lift the lamb out of the marinade and thread it onto the skewers.

Heat a griddle pan or heavy frying pan until it is very hot. Place the skewers on the griddle and cook for about 10 minutes, turning often and basting the lamb with the remaining marinade, until the lamb is just cooked.

Put the skewers on a warmed plate and leave them to rest for a few minutes. Serve with lemon wedges. *The picture also shows Sticky Rice Parcels (see page 58).*

Lisa's tip Leave the lamb slightly pink inside to keep the meat juicy. If you have time, leave the lamb in the marinade overnight for even more flavour. When cooking the skewers, keep turning them to prevent the spices from burning, otherwise they will leave a bitter taste.

MUTTON STEW WITH FLATBREADS

YANG ROU PAO MO 羊肉泡馍

SERVES 4

PREP TIME
30 MINUTES, PLUS
20 MINUTES FOR
THE FLATBREADS,
PLUS 1 HOUR RISING
COOK TIME
1 HOUR FOR
THE FLATBREADS,
1½ HOURS FOR
THE STEW

Xi'an's Terracotta Army is an awe-inspiring sight and what's incredible is that the soldiers they were modelled on, back in the third century BCE, probably enjoyed this dish. The stewed mutton with soaked bread (a bit like dumplings) is still hugely popular today, especially in the cold weather.

When I visited Xi'an it was freezing. My legs were numb with cold, we'd just come off a four-hour drive and I remember our guide calling, 'Helen, Lisa, come over here. I've found someone who can teach you this famous dish of Xi'an.' When I was presented with a bowl of this stew it looked simple, but the magic of the dish became apparent on tasting. I've often found mutton stringy and tough, but this dish was delightful and it enhanced my experience of Xi'an.

1kg/2lb 4oz mutton or lamb shoulder, in one piece

about 1 litre/1¾ pints/4 cups boiling water

5 garlic cloves, halved

3 shallots, halved

4 whole star anise

2 pieces of cassia bark or cinnamon sticks

2cm/¾in piece of fresh root ginger, sliced

3 large dried red chillies

2 tsp salt

Flatbreads

2 tbsp white sugar

200ml/7fl oz/generous ¾ cup warm water

1½ tsp dried yeast

375g/13oz/3 cups plain (all-purpose) flour, plus extra for dusting

1½ tsp baking powder

1 tbsp vegetable oil, plus extra for frying

To serve

200g/7oz rice vermicelli, soaked in hot water for 5 minutes, then drained

4–6 spring onions (scallions), diced

To make the flatbreads, mix the sugar, warm water and yeast in a small bowl. Sift the flour and baking powder together into a large bowl and add the vegetable oil. Gradually mix in the yeast mixture, then knead for 15 minutes until smooth. Put the dough in a bowl, cover with a damp tea towel and leave in a warm place for 1 hour until the dough has doubled in size.

Meanwhile, to make the mutton broth, place the meat in a large pan and add enough boiling water to just cover the meat. Add the garlic, shallots, star anise, cassia or cinnamon, ginger, chillies and salt and simmer gently for 1–1½ hours until the meat is tender. Transfer the meat to a chopping board and slice thinly. Skim and discard any froth from the surface of the broth.

Turn out the dough onto a lightly floured work surface and knead lightly. Divide the dough in half and shape each piece into a log, then divide each log into 6 equal pieces. Roll out each piece into an 8cm/3in square. Starting from the edge closest to you, roll the dough upwards until it looks like a log again. Next, coil it into a snail shape and tuck the end underneath. Using the rolling pin, roll out the dough to a disc about 5mm/¼in thick. Keeping the rolled-out dough covered with a damp tea towel, continue until you have made all 12 flatbreads. Leave to rest for 10 minutes.

Heat a frying pan over a high heat, add 2 tablespoons of vegetable oil and add a disc of dough. It will bubble and expand in the pan. Cook for 2–3 minutes on each side until golden brown. Repeat until all the flatbreads are cooked and set aside to cool.

To serve, heat the mutton broth in a wok, add the soaked vermicelli, the spring onions, and 3 or 4 slices of mutton per person. Break 6–10 flatbreads into little pieces and add to the broth. Simmer for 5 minutes, then serve in bowls.

Lisa's tip If you have leftover flatbread they will keep for a day or two in a plastic bag. Heat in the toaster or under the grill, then slice open like a pitta bread. Dice any leftover mutton with some of the juices and use to fill the flatbreads.

BEEF BALLS ON A STICK

NIU ROU WAN 牛丸串

Chinese meatballs are typically made of pork and can be steamed, boiled or deep-fried. A Cantonese variant, the steamed meatball, is made of beef and served as a dim sum or street snack. I remember when the makeshift food truck (a lorry which had a gas burner at the back of the open top) arrived in a village we were visiting not far from the city of Dongguan, and it was an undoubted thrill for the local folk. Adults felt like children, there was laughter in the street. Biting into one of these meatballs felt like the party had just begun.

300g/10½oz minced (ground) beef

40g/1½oz pork fat, finely chopped

1 piece of dried orange peel,
    soaked for 10 minutes,
    and finely chopped

2 water chestnuts, diced

1 tbsp finely chopped coriander
    (cilantro)

1 tsp soy sauce

1 tbsp oyster sauce

1 tsp Shaoxing rice wine

¼ tsp ground white pepper

¼ tsp sesame oil

1 tbsp potato starch

2 tbsp water

vegetable oil for greasing

Mix the beef, pork fat, orange peel, water chestnuts and coriander in a bowl. Season with the soy sauce, oyster sauce, wine, white pepper and sesame oil, then add the potato starch and water and mix well in a clockwise direction; the mixture will become paste-like.

Rub a drop of oil on the palms of your hands, scoop out 1 tablespoon of the mixture and shape into a perfectly round ball. Repeat until you have made 12 meatballs. Place the beef balls on an oiled plate.

Place a trivet or round cake rack in a wok and add boiling water so that it is just over a quarter full. Put the plate on top of the trivet, cover with a lid and steam for 10 minutes or until the beef balls are firm and fully cooked. Serve using wooden cocktail sticks or small wooden skewers.

Lisa's tip Ask your butcher for some pork fat: it loosens the beef mixture so it's lighter to bite into. If you don't want to use pork fat, you could use a similar amount of finely chopped aubergine or mushroom.

SERVES 4
(MAKES 12)

PREP TIME
20 MINUTES, PLUS
15 MINUTES RISING
COOK TIME
40 MINUTES

BEEF PANCAKE

NIU ROU XIAN BING 牛肉餡餅

This beef pancake is famous throughout China. I tried it in Xi'an and I can still recall the taste of of the first mouthful: absolutely divine. The beef juices are absorbed into the pancake, making every bite so satisfying and tasty. It's not surprising that there are many legends about this dish, which dates back to the time of the Tang dynasty. The Emperor Xuanzong is said to have disguised himself so that he could go to the small shop in Xi'an where these pancakes were made. And Bai Juyi, a famous poet of the Tang dynasty, wrote a poem about them, called 'Send the Pancake to Yang Wan Zhou'.

Dough

300g/10½oz/scant 2½ cups strong white bread flour, plus extra for dusting

50g/1¾oz/6 tbsp cornflour (corn starch)

1 tsp fast-acting dried yeast

1 tsp salt

175ml/6fl oz/¾ cup water

4 tbsp vegetable oil for frying

Beef filling

300g/10½oz minced (ground) beef

60g/2¼oz spring onions (scallions), finely chopped

1½ tsp salt

1 tbsp sesame oil

1 tbsp caster (superfine) sugar

pinch of ground white pepper

1 egg white

To make the filling, put all the ingredients into a bowl and mix together using your hand (wear disposable gloves if you don't like touching raw meat); gather the mixture together and slam it down into the bowl until it comes together (this breaks down the protein and softens it); do not put the mixture into a food processor as you do not want it too smooth. Cover the bowl with clingfilm and put it in the fridge while you prepare the pastry.

To make the dough, mix both flours, the yeast and water together and knead until it forms a smooth dough with a sheen. Gather the dough into a ball, put it in a bowl, cover with a damp tea towel or clingfilm and leave in a warm place to rest for 15 minutes (it will rise slightly).

Turn the dough out onto a lightly floured work surface. Shape the dough into a log and cut into 12 equal pieces. Using a rolling pin, roll each piece into a circle about 3mm/⅛in thick.

Place a circle of dough on the palm of your hand. Spoon on about 2 tablespoons of beef filling. Gather the dough at the top to cover the filling and press together to seal. Turn the dough upside down and pat into a pancake shape about 2cm/½in thick and 5cm/2in in diameter.

Cook the pancakes in two or three batches. Heat a frying pan over a high heat and add a little of the vegetable oil. Carefully place the pancakes in the pan and cook for about 3 minutes on each side. Turn the heat down to medium and cook for an additional 4–5 minutes on each side until golden brown.

Lisa's tip If you don't want to fry these pancakes, you can bake them in a preheated oven at 180°C/350°F/gas 4 for about 15–20 minutes. Brush them with beaten egg before baking to give them a glossy sheen.

BEEF JERKY

MI ZHI NIU 蜜汁牛

This Chinese-style dried meat is one of my favourite treats when I go to Hong Kong or Singapore. When I see it I have to stop whatever I am doing to buy a slice and eat it there and then. I remember in the heart of Tsim Sha Tsui in Hong Kong it was pouring with tropical rain and the road was covered by a sea of umbrellas. I told my sister to get off the tram as I had spotted the jerky shop.

'What, now?' said Lisa.

'I've waited ages to find that shop. Quick, get off the tram before we have to walk back one stop.'

We jumped off and I could hear my sister curse quietly. Dodging the umbrellas and half soaked, we got to the shop and pointed at the pork jerky. The lady in the shop began to wrap it and I said, 'No need, just pass it over.' I wolfed it down. I should really have eaten slowly and savoured the flavour but the anticipation was too much. Lisa was shaking her head at me. 'You are so embarrassing. It's like you've not eaten for years. Control yourself!'

This meat preservation technique originates from China. It is often made with beef, pork or mutton, which are prepared with spices, sugar, salt and soy sauce, and dried on racks at around 50–60°C/120–140°F. Jerky is very popular in Hong Kong, Singapore and Malaysia, where it is usually eaten during Chinese New Year. When Chinese immigrants brought this delicacy to Singapore and Malaysia, it began to take on local characteristics. In one version the meat, instead of being air-dried, is grilled over charcoal. This imparts a smokier flavour to the meat. I recreated this snack back home and was really pleased with the results. I made an extra slice for Lisa, just to make her laugh. However, blink and you've missed it. She enjoys these snacks as much as I do.

450g/1lb minced (ground) beef rump

Flavourings
2 tbsp Thai fish sauce
1½ tbsp light soy sauce
1½ tbsp dark soy sauce
1½ tbsp Shaoxing rice wine
100g/3½oz/½ cup brown sugar
1 tsp cayenne pepper
pinch of garlic powder
pinch of ground ginger

Glaze
2 tbsp clear honey
4 tbsp warm water

Place all the flavourings in a large bowl and stir well. Add the beef and mix in one direction for 5–10 minutes until it becomes paste-like.

Preheat the oven to 150°C/300°F/gas 2. Lay a large sheet of baking parchment on the work surface and tip the meat mixture onto the parchment. Cover with a piece of clingfilm and use a rolling pin to roll out the mixture into a thin sheet, approx. 3mm/⅛in thick. Remove the clingfilm and place the meat on the parchment onto a large baking sheet. Place in the oven for 15 minutes.

Once one side is cooked, peel the thin sheet of meat off the parchment and turn it over, placing it back on the parchment. Cook for a further 15 minutes.

Increase the oven temperature to 180°C/350°F/gas 4.

To glaze, dissolve the honey in the water. Remove the baking sheet from the oven and brush the honey glaze over the top of the meat. Return the jerky to the oven and cook for 5 minutes. Turn the jerky over and brush the other side with the honey glaze. Return the jerky to the oven and cook for a further 5 minutes.

Remove the jerky from the parchment paper and leave to cool on a wire rack. When cool, cut into small pieces. It can be stored in the fridge for up to 4–5 days.

Lisa's tip Instead of beef, try minced pork or a combination of beef and pork.

CHINESE BARBECUE

SHAOKAO 烧烤

From a foodie's perspective, Shanghai begins and ends on the street of Nanchang Lu. Everything in the world of food is there. Row upon row of tightly packed street vendors selling everything from roasted scorpions, caramelized fruit, dumplings, noodles, sticky rice and 24-herb tea to these *shaokao*. You can have breakfast, lunch, dinner, dessert and drinks as you walk along. The *shaokao* stand is heaving with hungry people who've made a detour to pick up some Chinese barbecue. Rows of bamboo skewers threaded with various meats and vegetables are thrown onto the charcoal grill, glistening with oil as the chilli powder glows bright red and wafts of Sichuan peppercorns makes someone sneeze a few stalls down.

My first hour in Shanghai was spent walking around this foodie paradise, each stand more seductive than the last. A man with piercing grey eyes smiled at me, coaxing me to try his food. He called out, 'Pretty girl, come and eat with me. These *shaokao* are the best.' How could I resist, despite already having eaten my fair share of *shaokao* farther up the road?

'Give me one, then,' I replied, and handed over a yuan. I wasn't disappointed. The chicken was sweet and tender with a hint of cumin. He raised his eyebrows expectantly, waiting for my verdict.

'I've travelled all the way from the UK for *shaokao* and yours are the best.'

'Thank you!' The man grinned, exposing a row of missing front teeth. Then he asked why I was so far from home.

'To eat. To find street food like yours,' I responded.

He laughed and laughed. Finally he took a deep breath and handed me a free *shaokao*. 'If you were my daughter,' he said, 'I'd never let you go.'

500g/1lb 2oz skinless, boneless chicken thighs

1 tsp salt

5 tbsp vegetable oil

2 tsp sesame oil

2 tsp chilli oil (optional)

Spice mix
½ tsp garlic powder

½ tsp ground cumin

½ tsp ground coriander

½ tsp onion powder

½ tsp paprika

½ tsp dried chilli flakes

2 tsp caster (superfine) sugar

½ tsp salt

Soak 10 wooden skewers in water for 30 minutes.

Butterfly each chicken thigh and slice into 2cm/¾in wide x 6cm/2½in long strips. Season the chicken with the salt. Thread two chicken strips concertina-style onto each skewer, leaving the bottom of the skewer clear. Brush about half of the vegetable oil and sesame oil over the chicken.

Mix together all the ingredients for the spice mix.

Heat a griddle pan or heavy frying pan until it is very hot. Place the skewers on the griddle and cook for about 4–6 minutes, sprinkling about half the spice mix over them as they cook. Turn the skewers, sprinkle with the remaining spice mix and brush with the remaining vegetable oil – or with chilli oil for a spicier result – and cook for another 4–6 minutes. When the chicken is cooked through, serve hot.

Illustrated overleaf.

Lisa's tips If you like, garnish by sprinkling some toasted sesame seeds over the cooked chicken. I prefer to use chicken thigh because it has a deeper flavour and chewier texture, but you could use chicken breast meat. Alternatively, use rump steak or pork loin. As a vegetarian option try skewers of courgettes, aubergines, peppers, mushrooms and pressed tofu, either individually or mixed.

FRIED CHICKEN LEGS

ZHA JI TUI 炸雞腿

The area of Mong Kok in Hong Kong preserves its traditional character with an array of markets, small shops and food stalls that have disappeared from other areas over the past several decades of economic development and urban transformation. I love the Ladies' Market in Mong Kok but it will always remind me of fried chicken leg. I felt rather shady queuing for one of these guilty pleasures and when I bit into the crispy chicken skin my tongue and taste buds rejoiced – and at the same time my brain felt a twinge of regret because of the calorie content. But I was in travel mode and it seemed a bit harsh to restrict myself. I had no choice that day but to look beyond the scales of the everyday and think of bigger things – like the best fried chicken leg I've ever tasted! Needless to say I had a good old chat with the vendor and he was kind enough to share this recipe with me. The longer you marinate the chicken the more flavour this dish will have. If you can leave it overnight it makes a huge difference.

4 chicken legs

2 tbsp finely chopped garlic

½ tsp Chinese five-spice powder

1 tbsp soy sauce

1 tsp salt

5 tbsp potato starch

vegetable oil for deep-frying

Put the chicken legs in a bowl with the garlic, five-spice powder, soy sauce and salt. Leave to marinate for 10 minutes or as long as you can – preferably overnight.

Dust the marinated chicken legs in the potato starch.

Heat a deep-fat fryer or a large deep saucepan over a high heat and add the oil. When it begins to smoke, add the chicken legs and turn frequently until all sides are browned and slightly crisp. After 3 minutes, turn the heat to medium and cook for an additional 10–15 minutes until the chicken is cooked through. Drain on paper towels and serve immediately.

Lisa's tip When deep-frying, cook in batches to prevent the oil's temperature from dropping. If you don't have a deep-fat fryer, cook two chicken legs at a time in a large deep saucepan or wok. Never leave the pan when deep-frying as this may result in a fire in the kitchen.

BRAISED OFFAL

HONG SHAO NIU ZA 紅燒牛雜

SERVES 4

PREP TIME
15 MINUTES
COOK TIME
2–3 HOURS

Nose-to-tail eating has recently become trendy in some of Britain's top restaurants. However, in China, as in France, no part of the animal is wasted. There is a Chinese saying that 'The Chinese will eat anything with four legs with its back to the skies except tables and chairs.' Offal dishes are particularly popular in the southern province of Guangdong and in Hong Kong.

My family originate from Guangzhou, the capital of Guangdong, and when I returned to my roots I had to try their speciality of braised offal. All around me in the makeshift café sit patrons on plastic stools feeding frantically as if they've discovered a rare treat. Offal has a punchy flavour, and the great knots and tangle of intestines, if treated with low heat and liquid, break down into soft, silken strands. When I bite into this delicacy I can feel the distinctive texture on my tongue. It's delicious as long as you don't spend too long thinking about what bits of the animal you are actually eating.

The types of offal used in this dish are normally beef stomach (tripe), beef or pig's tongue, pig's or sheep's hearts, and chicken livers. I would encourage you to try this dish: the offal absorbs the flavours so well and makes a delicious delicacy.

500g/1lb 2oz offal of your choice, such as tripe, ox or pig's tongue, chicken hearts or chicken livers

4 tsp salt

3 tbsp vegetable oil

600ml/20fl oz/2½ cups chicken stock

2 tbsp dark soy sauce

4 tbsp Shaoxing rice wine

3 tsp brown sugar

Braising spices

3cm/1¼in piece of fresh root ginger, sliced

4 garlic cloves, peeled

1 cinnamon stick

2–3 star anise

1 black cardamom pod

4 cloves

1 tsp fennel seeds

3 bay leaves

Wash the offal thoroughly in cold water. Drain and mix with the salt. If you are cooking ox tongue, simmer in a large pan of water until the tongue is tender, then drain and slice.

Heat a large deep saucepan over a medium heat and add the oil. Add the ginger, garlic cloves and the remaining braising spices and fry for a few minutes. Add the offal and the stock and bring to the boil; the spices will create a fragrant stock. Reduce the heat, add the soy sauce, wine and sugar and simmer gently for 2–3 hours until the offal is very tender.

NOTE: If you are cooking chicken livers simmer for only 20–30 minutes, otherwise they will become very rubbery.

Serve the offal in a bowl with some of the stock (leave the spices in the pan).

KOREAN FRIED CHICKEN

HAN GUO ZHA JI 韓國炸雞

SERVES 4

PREP TIME
25 MINUTES
COOK TIME
25 MINUTES

Chinese people will proudly tell you that their fried chicken is the best. But arguably that was before Korean fried chicken came onto the scene, offering an eggshell-thin, ultra-crisp crust around a drippingly juicy interior.

I met a taxi driver in Hong Kong. Mr Wu was a short, blunt-speaking man with an air of arrogance about him. His greying hair had been combed to cover his bald patch, but this accentuated his sticking-out ears. He was confident in his views and so was I. We came close to having an argument as to whether the best fried chicken was the Hong Kong style or the Korean style. Eventually, he stopped the meter and drove me to a Korean fried chicken joint to try a portion of wings and thighs. He won the wager. Credit to him, as he introduced me to something new and – I have to to admit – amazingly good. I had to hand it to the Koreans. Their K-pop and K-dramas have achieved cult status and so too has their fried chicken.

I've tried many different methods to make this fried chicken, but the recipe below is the one I think gives the best results. The secret is in the crispiness of the chicken from the double coating of batter. If you have time, it is best to prepare this the day before so the chicken can marinate overnight.

4 chicken drumsticks or thighs (or 8 wings)

about 12 tbsp potato starch or cornflour (corn starch)

2 eggs, beaten

vegetable oil for deep-frying

sesame seeds, to garnish

pickles, to serve (optional)

Marinade
1 tbsp salt

1 tbsp garlic powder

1 tbsp onion powder

2 tbsp cold water

Sauce
2 tbsp vegetable oil

2 tbsp finely sliced garlic

2 tsp dried chilli flakes

2 fresh chillies, finely chopped (optional)

10 tbsp water

4 tbsp brown sugar

3 tbsp chopped peanuts (optional)

1 tbsp rice wine vinegar

1 tbsp soy sauce

½ tsp potato starch

Put the chicken in a bowl, add all the marinade ingredients and mix well. Leave in the fridge to marinate for 10 minutes or as long as you can – preferably overnight.

Dip the chicken pieces in the potato starch and shake off any excess. Dip the chicken in the beaten egg and then re-coat the chicken in potato starch.

Half-fill a wok or saucepan with vegetable oil. Heat the oil to 180°C/350°F; if you don't have a cooking thermometer, test by dipping a wooden chopstick or wooden spoon into the oil – if bubbles immediately form around the chopstick the oil is hot enough. Add the chicken and reduce the heat to low–medium. Deep-fry for 15–20 minutes until golden brown and the chicken is cooked through: to test, pierce the flesh with a thin skewer and if the juices run clear the chicken is done. Drain on paper towels.

To make the sauce, heat the vegetable oil in a saucepan over a medium heat and fry the garlic and chillies for 1 minute. Then add the water, sugar and all the remaining ingredients and stir until the sauce thickens. Remove from the heat, add the chicken and mix well to coat all the pieces in the sauce. Because the chicken has been double coated it will not go soggy, and when you bite in the chicken will still be moist and juicy. Sprinkle with sesame seeds and serve with pickles of your choice.

Lisa's tip I think this dish goes particularly well with a cold beer – it brings out the sweetness of the chicken.

Adjust the spiciness according to your taste. If you like it extra spicy then add some finely chopped bird's eye chillies to the sauce.

SERVES 4

PREP TIME
1½ HOURS, PLUS
1 HOUR MARINATING
COOK TIME
2 HOURS

BEGGAR'S CHICKEN

JIAO HUA JI 叫化鸡

In this dish the chicken is stuffed, wrapped in dough, and baked. The name of the dish comes from an old story about a beggar who had stolen a chicken and didn't want anyone to know he was cooking it, so he covered the chicken in mud, hoping that the smell of the cooked chicken wouldn't escape. This method made the chicken even tastier and more tender. As the beggar was tucking in, a passing nobleman smelt the chicken and asked to try it. The beggar shared the chicken with him and it was so good that the nobleman asked how to make the dish. That is how this dish made its way to the Imperial Court. Today, 'beggar's chicken' is considered a staple of Chinese haute cuisine, and it is now often wrapped in lotus leaves before baking. Some recipes call for the lotus-wrapped chicken to be covered in clay or a flour-based dough to seal in the juices. Some still even cook this dish outdoors over hot coals. Despite its lengthy cooking process, it always sells out.

1 whole chicken, about 1.5kg/3lb 5oz

3 large dried lotus leaves and string (or use foil or a plastic roasting bag)

Salt dough
500g/1lb 2oz/4 cups plain (all-purpose) flour

500g/1lb 2oz/1¾ cups salt

200ml/7fl oz/generous ¾ cup cold water

Marinade
3 whole star anise

3 tbsp light soy sauce

3 tbsp Shaoxing rice wine

3 tbsp sesame oil

Stuffing
4 tbsp vegetable oil

3 onions, diced

3 garlic cloves, finely sliced or grated

200g/7oz pork tenderloin, diced small

3 spring onions (scallions), cut into 3cm/1¼in pieces

10 medium-sized dried shiitake mushrooms, soaked in hot water for 20 minutes, then finely sliced

3 tbsp light soy sauce

3 tbsp Shaoxing rice wine

½ tsp salt

½ tsp ground white pepper

Mix the marinade ingredients in a large bowl. Add the chicken and turn it around to cover with the marinade. Cover the bowl with clingfilm and leave in the fridge to marinate for 1 hour – or preferably overnight.

To make the stuffing, heat a wok over a high heat and add the vegetable oil. Add the onions and garlic and cook for 1 minute. Add the pork and cook over a high heat for 5 minutes (the pork doesn't need to be fully cooked at this stage). Then add the spring onions and shiitake mushrooms, soy sauce, wine, salt and pepper and cook for an additional 5 minutes. Put the stuffing in a bowl to cool slightly.

Make the salt dough in a separate bowl: mix the flour, salt and water together to form a dough. (The salt will not make the chicken intensely salty, it will just harden the dough when cooking.)

If you are using lotus leaves to wrap the chicken, put the dried leaves into a bowl of hot water to soak for about 10 minutes.

Preheat the oven to 200°/400°F/gas 6.

Take the chicken out of the marinade and remove the star anise. Stuff the chicken with the stuffing. Drain the lotus leaves, if using. Wrap the chicken in lotus leaves and tie with string, or alternatively wrap in foil, ensuring that there are no gaps, or place in a roasting bag. Now cover the wrapped chicken with the dough; the dough should be about 1cm/½in thick. Put the chicken in a baking dish and bake for 2 hours.

To serve, break open the dough and discard (it is not to be eaten). Transfer the chicken to a serving plate and carefully unwrap it. Serve with the stuffing.

Lisa's tip The lotus leaves impart a fragrant aroma to the chicken. Once the dough is opened up the chicken will just fall off the bones.

SERVES 4

PREP TIME
25 MINUTES
COOK TIME
25 MINUTES

SALT AND PEPPER FRIED CHICKEN

XIAN SU JI 椒鹽雞

The name of this dish stems from the five-spice powder, which includes Sichuan peppercorns. I remember sharing a portion of this with my sister when we were in Guangzhou and we thought it was ingenious because we'd only seen chicken cubes used for sweet and sour chicken. We've debated long and hard about which recipe is better: we think that, by a very narrow margin, salt and pepper chicken is a winner.

400g/14oz skinless, boneless chicken
  breasts, cut into 3cm/1¼in cubes

1 tsp salt

1 tsp caster (superfine) sugar

1 tbsp potato starch or cornflour (corn
  starch), plus about 6 tbsp for coating

3 tbsp water

vegetable oil for deep-frying

1 small onion, finely sliced

1 green pepper, deseeded and finely sliced

1 garlic clove, finely chopped

1 fresh red chilli, finely sliced

Salt and pepper mix

½ tsp ground ginger

½ tsp Chinese five-spice powder

1 tsp caster (superfine) sugar

½ tsp salt

Put the chicken in a bowl, add the salt, sugar, potato starch and water and stir to combine evenly. Cover the bowl with clingfilm and put in the fridge for about 10 minutes to marinate.

Mix all the ingredients for the salt and pepper mix in a small bowl and set aside.

Half-fill a wok or large saucepan with vegetable oil. Heat the oil to 180°C/350°F; if you don't have a cooking thermometer, test by dipping a wooden chopstick or wooden spoon into the oil – if bubbles immediately form around the chopstick the oil is hot enough.

Put about 6 tablespoons of potato starch in a shallow bowl. Dip each cube of chicken into the potato starch and turn to coat on all sides. Deep-fry the chicken in the hot oil for 5 minutes until golden brown. Lift out with a slotted spoon and drain on paper towels.

Pour off the oil into a metal container. Put 1 tablespoon of the oil back into the wok over a high heat, add the onion, pepper, garlic and chilli and stir-fry for about 3 minutes until the onion is translucent. Return the chicken cubes to the wok, sprinkle over the spice mix and toss together. Serve immediately.

Lisa's tips Instead of chicken, you could make this with tofu, mushrooms or squid.

If you have guests who don't like it too spicy, omit the fresh chilli.

STEAMED CHICKEN AND MUSHROOMS ON RICE

ZHENG WU JI HE MO GU 蒸烏雞和蘑菇

SERVES 4

PREP TIME
40 MINUTES,
PLUS 30 MINUTES
MARINATING
COOK TIME
1 HOUR 20 MINUTES

The silkie (sometimes spelled silky) is a breed of chicken named for its fluffy plumage, which is said to feel like silk. (Marco Polo wrote about a 'furry chicken' during his travels in Asia in the 13th century.) The breed has several other unusual qualities, such as black skin and bones and greyish-black meat.

The best way to cook a silkie is to steam it over rice in a bamboo log. I first tried this wonderful dish when I was at mid-point climbing a rice paddy and stopped off at a small café for lunch. The bamboo log was filled with rice and black chicken pieces, the meat was falling off the bone and the steaming process created intense flavours from the juices of the chicken. The texture of the flesh is smoother and the flavour is denser than that of an ordinary chicken, but if you haven't got a silkie then normal chicken is fine for this recipe. And for those who don't have bamboo logs to hand, don't worry, we've adapted the recipe. In this simple recipe, all the ingredients steam together in a big bowl; it's a healthy way to cook chicken.

1 silkie chicken, cut into 12 pieces

10 dried Chinese mushrooms, soaked in hot
    water for 20 minutes, then cut into halves

500g/1lb 2oz/2¾ cups jasmine rice

1 tbsp sesame oil

1 spring onion (scallion), finely sliced,
    to garnish

Marinade
4 x 3cm/1¼in slices of fresh root ginger

2 tbsp light soy sauce

2 tsp dark soy sauce

2 tsp caster (superfine) sugar

2 tbsp potato starch or cornflour
    (corn starch)

2 tbsp Shaoxing rice wine

Mix the marinade ingredients in a large heatproof bowl. Add the chicken pieces and mushrooms and mix well. Cover the bowl with clingfilm and leave in the fridge to marinate for 30 minutes.

Wash the rice in a sieve under cold running water and drain well. Repeat this three times or until the water is no longer cloudy. Tip the drained rice into a bowl that will fit in a steamer or a wok and add water to cover the rice by about 5cm/2in.

Place a trivet or round cake rack in a wok and add boiling water so that it is just over a quarter full. Place the bowl of rice inside a large bamboo steamer (if you have one) or directly on top of the trivet. Cover with a lid and steam over a high heat for 10 minutes. The rice will have absorbed half of the water at this point.

Open the lid and add the chicken pieces and mushrooms to the rice. Pour the remaining marinade over the chicken and rice. Cover with the lid and continue to steam for 1 hour over low–medium heat until the chicken is cooked through. To serve, drizzle the sesame oil and sprinkle the spring onion on top.

Lisa's tip Any leftovers can be eaten the next day and will be even more delicious as the flavours will have fully absorbed into the rice. You can swap the white rice for brown or red rice if you wish.

SERVES 4 (MAKES
8 SKEWERS)

PREP TIME
10 MINUTES,
PLUS 20 MINUTES
MARINATING
COOK TIME
15 MINUTES

CHICKEN SATAY

SHA CHA JI ROU 沙爹雞

Satay is a simple dish of seasoned, skewered and grilled meat, served with a sauce. But it's the mildly spicy, peanut-based sauce that makes the satay. It is thought to originate from Javanese street vendors who adapted Indian kebabs, making them smaller and using different spices. Across the hawker stalls of Hong Kong, satay is a firm favourite, usually sold side by side with Fishballs (page 65).

400g/14oz chicken fillets, cut into
   10cm/4in strips

Marinade
1 tbsp sesame oil
1 tbsp Shaoxing rice wine or sherry
1 tbsp light soy sauce
½ tsp salt
½ tsp caster (superfine) sugar
½ tbsp finely chopped garlic

Peanut sauce
140g/5oz/1 cup raw unsalted peanuts
1 tbsp vegetable oil
½ tsp salt
½ tsp ground turmeric
½ tsp chilli paste
1–2 tbsp soft brown sugar
150–200ml/5–7fl oz/about ¾ cup water

Soak 8 wooden skewers, approx. 18cm/7in long, in water for 30 minutes.

Mix the marinade ingredients in a bowl, add the chicken and coat all over. Cover the bowl with clingfilm and leave in the fridge to marinate for about 20 minutes.

To make the peanut sauce, crush the peanuts using a pestle and mortar; alternatively put them in a plastic bag and crush them with a rolling pin. Don't put them in a food processor, otherwise they will be too finely ground. Put a saucepan over a medium heat (without any oil), add the peanuts and toast for about 3 minutes until browned. Add the oil, salt, turmeric, chilli paste, sugar to taste, and 150ml/5fl oz/ ⅔ cup water, and cook over a low heat for 5 minutes. Add a little more water if necessary. Set aside in a bowl until ready to serve.

Thread the chicken onto the skewers.

Heat a griddle pan until it is very hot. Place the skewers on the griddle and cook for 3 minutes on each side until golden brown and the chicken is cooked through. Serve hot, with the peanut sauce.

Lisa's tip These can also be cooked in a moderate oven 180°C/350°F/gas 4 or on a charcoal barbecue.

STICKY RICE PARCELS

ZÒNGZI 粽子

MAKES 6

PREP TIME
50 MINUTES, PLUS
OVERNIGHT SOAKING
COOK TIME
4 HOURS

During the Dragon Boat Festival the Chinese people eat *zòngzi* to honour the patriotic poet and politician Qu Yuán – who drowned himself in the river when his country perished in the Warring States period, an era of ancient Chinese history. It is said that people threw rice dumplings wrapped in bamboo leaves into the river to keep the fish away from Qu Yuán's body. It is traditional to eat *zòngzi* on the fifth day of the fifth month of the Chinese lunar calendar, which usually falls in early to mid-June.

Today, people usually use reed or bamboo leaves (which are not eaten) as the wrapping for *zòngzi*. (You can buy bamboo leaves from Chinese grocers.) The sticky rice filling may include meat, beans or bean paste, mushrooms, Chinese dates or walnuts. Some regions have an even greater diversity.

When my grandmother used to visit from Hong Kong around the time of the Dragon Boat Festival, she'd take it upon herself to make as many *zòngzi* as possible, getting all of us involved in the assembly line. One of us would be in charge of scooping the rice, another the fillings, and my grandmother completed the task by binding them tightly so the filling wouldn't fall out when boiling them up. I remember one year we had a bit of a competition and ended up making so many we were still eating them at Christmas!

600g/1lb 5oz/3¼ cups glutinous rice, washed, then soaked in water overnight

300g/10½oz/1½ cups dried mung beans, soaked in water overnight

100g/3½oz dried chestnuts, soaked in hot water for 1 hour, or canned chestnuts

15 dried black mushrooms, soaked in hot water for 15 minutes

300g/10½oz chicken or pork, sliced

1 tbsp salt

⅛ tsp Chinese five-spice powder

12–15 bamboo leaves

soy sauce, to serve

Drain the rice, beans, chestnuts and mushrooms. Chop the chestnuts. Cut the stalks off the mushrooms and cut into slices. Mix the chicken or pork with the salt and five-spice powder.

Place two pieces of kitchen string, each about 40cm/16in long, on your work surface. Put two bamboo leaves on top, slightly overlapping, at right angles to the string so it is ready to tie.

Put a handful of rice (about 80g/2¾oz/scant ½ cup) in the middle of each leaf, then add 50g/1¾oz of mung beans. Now add some of the chicken or pork, chestnuts and mushrooms. Cover the mound with a bit more rice (about 1½ tablespoons). Fold the bamboo leaves over as if wrapping a present and use the string to tie the parcel firmly. Make five more parcels in the same way.

Place the parcels in a large pan of cold water and bring to the boil. Reduce the heat to low and simmer for 4 hours.

Drain and serve the *zòngzi* with soy sauce. *Also illustrated on page 39.*

Lisa's tip One of my favourite ingredients which you could add to each *zòngzi* is a salty duck's egg yolk. These are sold in all Chinese grocery stores.

FISH AND SEAFOOD

鱼和海鲜

HOT AND SOUR SOUP

LA TANG 辣湯

This soup is based on the flavours of Sichuan: hot, sour, spicy and delicious, a perfect balance of flavours and textures. It certainly wakes up the senses and clears the sinuses.

600ml/20fl oz/2½ cups chicken stock

100g/3½oz skinless, firm white fish fillet, cut into small chunks

100g/3½oz small cooked peeled prawns (shrimp)

50g/1¾oz dried Chinese mushrooms, soaked in hot water for 20 minutes, then cut into strips

50g/1¾oz bamboo shoots

50g/1¾oz carrot, cut into strips

50g/1¾oz tofu, cut into strips

2 tbsp chilli bean paste

1 tbsp white vinegar

1 tbsp sugar

1 tsp salt

2 tbsp potato starch mixed with 2 tbsp cold water

1 egg, beaten

Pour the stock into a wok or saucepan and bring to the boil. Add the fish, prawns, mushrooms, bamboo shoots, carrot strips and tofu and simmer for 4 minutes, stirring now and again. Mix in the chilli bean paste and vinegar. Season with sugar and salt, stir well and cook for about 5 minutes until boiling.

Once the soup is boiling, add the potato starch mixture and mix in vigorously – if you don't stir the soup, it will become gloopy in the centre and watery around the edges. Turn off the heat and swirl in the beaten egg, stirring in a clockwise direction to ensure the soup has swirls of egg throughout. Serve in a bowl – a hot spicy soup, perfect for the cold weather.

Lisa's tips If you can't find chilli bean paste, substitute chilli sauce to taste.

If you love seafood you can add scallops, diced king prawns or oysters.

WHOLE YELLOW CROAKER FISH

HUÁNGYÚ 黃魚串

This dish is a feast for the eyes. It's rare in the Western world to see fish skewered from head to tail – but it shows the splendour of the fish, even with its bulging eyes. A small yellow croaker is the perfect size and texture to barbecue or bake whole. It's particularly lucky to enjoy this dish during Chinese New Year because the word for fish, yu, sounds like the words for 'wish' and 'abundance'; and also because the head and tail symbolize a good beginning to the New Year and a good ending to the year just gone. In China the fish is skewered for ease of eating as street food but for home cooking I have omitted the skewer. *Illustrated overleaf.*

1 whole yellow croaker fish (approx. 500g/1lb 2oz), or any smallish whole white fish such as sea bass, descaled and gutted

2 tbsp vegetable oil

1 tsp salt

¼ tsp Chinese five-spice powder

1 tsp garlic powder

¼ tsp ground ginger

3 spring onions (scallions), sliced into 3cm/1¼in pieces

Score the fish at an angle from head to tail, making cuts approx. 2cm/¾in apart – not too deep – to help the fish cook all the way through.

Rub the fish all over with vegetable oil, then season with the salt, five-spice powder, garlic powder, ginger and some spring onion pieces.

Heat the barbecue or oven grill, or preheat the oven to 150°C/300°F/gas 2. Cook the fish on the barbecue over a low–medium heat, or under the grill, for about 10 minutes on each side or until the fish is fully cooked. Alternatively cook in the oven for 15–20 minutes. Serve garnished with the remaining spring onions.

FISHBALLS IN CURRY

GA LI YU WAN 咖哩魚丸

SERVES 4
(MAKES 16)

PREP TIME
20 MINUTES, PLUS
30 MINUTES RESTING
COOK TIME
20 MINUTES

These are an institution of Hong Kong street food. They're the equivalent in popularity of a kebab after a night out on the town in the UK. The fishballs – which sometimes include prawns and spices – are cooked in a spicy curry broth which they absorb, so every bite is oozing in curry deliciousness. If you don't like curry, you can boil the fishballs in stock or water and have them with a dipping sauce such as sweet chilli. *Illustrated overleaf.*

600g/1lb 5oz skinless, firm white fish fillet, such as cod, haddock, hake, sea bass or halibut

1 egg white

2 tsp salt

3 tbsp potato starch or cornflour (corn starch)

400ml/14fl oz/1⅔ cups chicken or fish stock

20g/¾oz/3 tbsp curry powder

1 tsp sugar

pinch of chilli powder (optional)

100ml/3½fl oz/scant ½ cup coconut milk

Put the fish, egg white, 1 teaspoon of the salt and the potato starch in a food processor and blitz to a smooth paste, thinning it with 1–2 tablespoons of water if necessary.

Transfer the mixture into a bowl. Wet your hand with cold water and scoop up the mixture, then throw it back into the bowl. This helps break down the protein and makes the finished fishballs smoother – it also helps to relieve stress! Do this ten times, then put the mixture in the fridge for up to 30 minutes to firm up.

Shape the mixture into 16 golf-ball-sized balls.

To cook the fishballs, pour the stock into a saucepan and bring to the boil over a high heat. Add the fishballs and simmer for 10 minutes, gently turning them around in the pan. Using a slotted spoon, lift the fishballs out of the stock and keep warm.

Ladle a little of the stock into a separate saucepan over a medium heat and blend with the curry powder, the remaining salt and the sugar; if you want it extra hot, add the chilli powder. Mix thoroughly until the curry powder has blended in, then add the coconut milk and enough stock to achieve a thin soup-like consistency.

Add the fishballs to the curry sauce and heat through for 5 minutes. To serve, spoon four fishballs into each soup bowl with the curry stock.

Lisa's tip Instead of 600g fish, you could use 400g/14oz fish and 200g/7oz peeled raw prawns (shrimp).

Fishballs can be made in advance and frozen uncooked. When freezing, ensure that they are separated so that they retain their ball shape. To cook from frozen, boil them in hot water for about 20 minutes, then transfer into the curry stock and simmer for 5–10 minutes.

SERVES 4

PREP TIME
10 MINUTES, PLUS
1 HOUR MARINATING
COOK TIME
5 MINUTES

GRILLED SQUID

KAO YOU YU 烤魷魚

There is something particularly satisfying about biting into grilled squid. You get smokiness, the almost al dente texture and notes of sweetness. Squid is a great sustainable fish that is perfect to cook very quickly. Get your grill as hot as possible so the squid gets those char marks without overcooking.

500g/1lb 2oz squid with tentacles, cleaned, bodies left whole or cut into strips

grated zest of 1 lemon, juice of ¼ lemon

¼ tsp Chinese five-spice powder

2 garlic cloves, finely chopped

1 tsp salt

1 tsp sesame oil

2 tbsp vegetable oil

small handful of fresh coriander (cilantro), chopped

In a bowl, mix the squid with the lemon juice and zest, five-spice powder, garlic, salt and sesame oil. Leave to marinate for at least 10 minutes or up to 1 hour – the longer you marinate the more tender the squid will be, as the lemon juice breaks down the chewy texture of the flesh.

When you are ready to cook the squid, add the vegetable oil to the bowl and turn to coat the squid in the oil.

Heat a griddle pan over a high heat or heat your grill to high. When it is very hot, put the squid onto the griddle or grill and cook for 5 minutes, occasionally pressing the squid down with a spatula so it chars, and turning the tentacles frequently until they are cooked. To serve, sprinkle with coriander and a little more salt, if required.

Lisa's tip If you are using larger pieces of squid, score them in a lattice pattern before marinating to help them cook evenly.

FISH CONGEE

YU ZHOU 魚粥

Fish congee (rice porridge) was something that we grew up with and as children we usually had this either for breakfast or when we were ill. It can be made plain and totally tasteless – which is the best way if you are feeling under the weather. To add flavour, fish is a perfect option as it has a delicate taste and a flaky texture that marries well with the congee.

180g/6oz/1 cup long-grain rice

1.5 litres/2½ pints/6 cups water

250g/9oz white fish fillet,
cut into 2cm/¾in cubes

1 tsp salt

½ tsp sugar

1 garlic clove, finely chopped

1 small slice of fresh root ginger
(optional)

1 tsp Shaoxing rice wine

1 tsp potato starch

3 spring onions (scallions),
finely chopped

dash of light soy sauce

Wash the rice in a sieve under cold running water and drain well. Repeat this three times or until the water is no longer cloudy. Put the rice in a large saucepan with the measured water and cook over a low–medium heat for about 30 minutes, stirring occasionally.

Add the fish to the rice, together with the salt, sugar, garlic, ginger, wine and potato starch and cook for an additional 1 hour, stirring occasionally.

By the end of the cooking time, the rice will have broken to a silky, porridge-like consistency. Season to taste with more salt if necessary and serve in bowls, sprinkled with spring onions and a dash of soy sauce.

Lisa's tip You can replace the water with chicken stock to make the porridge more flavoursome.

QINGDAO SEA URCHIN

QING DAO HAI DAN 青島海膽

Qingdao is a large city on the coast of Shandong province, famous for its seafood. Some call sea urchin the 'king of the sea', so don't let the prickly shell put you off: this is its natural defence against predators. Inside you'll find the edible orange parts, which are creamy in texture, with a savoury umami taste, briny yet sweet and intensely rich – a 'must-try' if you are in Qingdao. Best served raw, sashimi-style, with wasabi and soy sauce.

12 fresh sea urchins

1 tbsp wasabi paste

2 tbsp light soy sauce

To open the sea urchins, hold them with a thick cloth and use a pair of scissors to cut a hole in the underside: find the mouth – a small opening – and follow the circle around. Shake out and discard the dark innards: the edible orange parts cling to the shell. Scoop out the orange parts and dip briefly in salted water to rinse, then serve with the wasabi and soy sauce.

Lisa's tip Only open the sea urchins immediately before you are going to eat them. And they must be fresh. Like oysters.

SERVES 4

PREP TIME
15 MINUTES
COOK TIME
10 MINUTES

PRAWN WONTON SOUP

XIA HUN DUN 蝦餛飩

Prawn wontons are a staple of dim sum menus across the world. A simple prawn paste is wrapped in small, thin pastry wrappers. They are then boiled to make a classic wonton soup, which may also include noodles. These prawn wontons can also be deep-fried and served with sweet and sour sauce.

250g/9oz raw king prawns (shrimp), peeled and deveined

1 tsp light soy sauce

½ tsp salt

½ tsp sugar

1 egg, beaten

½ tsp sesame oil

1 tsp potato starch

12 wonton wrappers

500ml/18fl oz/2 cups chicken stock

1 spring onion (scallion), finely chopped

In a food processor, blend the prawns with the soy sauce, salt, sugar, egg, sesame oil and potato starch.

Place 1 tablespoon of the prawn mixture in the centre of a wonton wrapper. Dab the edges of the wrapper with water and fold over into a triangle. Press to seal the edges, then fold the left and right corners towards the centre to create the shape of a bishop's mitre.

Cook the wontons in a saucepan of boiling water for 5–7 minutes, until firm to the touch, then drain.

Heat the chicken stock until it is boiling and add a drop of light soy sauce. Add the cooked wontons and simmer for 3 minutes. Serve hot, sprinkled with chopped spring onion.

Lisa's tip To make wonton noodle soup, soak thin dried egg noodles (allow one nest per person) in freshly boiled water for 5–7 minutes, then drain and place in a large bowl. Add to the soup with the cooked wontons. Garnish with either thinly sliced pak choi or spring onion.

SERVES 4, OR 2
AS A MAIN COURSE

PREP TIME
20 MINUTES
COOK TIME
15 MINUTES

SPRING ONION OIL NOODLES WITH DRIED SHRIMP

XIA MI CONG YOU MIAN 蝦米蔥油面

This is the stuff of breakfast, brunch and supper in Hong Kong and China. The simplicity of this dish is partly what makes it so appealing, but it's also the taste: the noodles absorb all the flavours of the spring onions and dried shrimp, making every bite super-delicious.

When I lived in Hong Kong I used to run down the steps of Wan Chai towards the little shop on the corner to get a bowl of these noodles on my way to work. Once I had the bowl of noodles in my hand I couldn't run, so any extra minutes I gained in advance could be used to slurp down this wonderful meal.

3 tbsp vegetable oil

100g/3½oz dried shrimp, soaked in warm water for 20 minutes, drained

4 nests of dried egg noodles, soaked in hot water for 5 minutes, drained

2 tbsp light soy sauce

1 tbsp Shaoxing rice wine

1 tbsp oyster sauce

1 tsp sesame oil

3 spring onions (scallions), finely chopped

dash of chilli oil (optional)

Heat a wok over a high heat, add the vegetable oil and fry the shrimp for about 1 minute – the shrimp will flavour the oil. Then add the noodles and stir vigorously so they don't stick. Season with soy sauce, wine, oyster sauce and sesame oil.

Serve in bowls and sprinkle with the spring onions. If you like it spicy, add some chilli oil to liven up these noodles.

Lisa's tip To ensure the noodles retain their springy texture, don't boil them or they will go soggy. Bring the water to the boil in a saucepan, then turn off the heat and add the noodles. Soak them for 5 minutes or so until softened, then drain and rinse in cold water to stop the cooking process. Drain again and your noodles are ready to cook.

CRAYFISH

XIAO LONG XIA 小龍蝦

I first came across these Hunan-style crayfish at Gui Jie, which translates as Ghost Street, in Beijing. Lisa and I squealed with delight at finding baby lobsters. We were quickly corrected by the vendor, who gave us a lecture on the difference between crayfish and lobsters. Crayfish are freshwater shellfish and although they have no meat in their claws, he preferred them as they had a sweeter, more delicate flavour. He swore by a dipping sauce of soy sauce, garlic, chilli and sesame oil and he said that if trade was slow he could eat the entire box of crayfish because the dipping sauce was so good. This recipe is dedicated to that vendor we met so many years ago. *Illustrated overleaf.*

32 large live crayfish

2 tbsp vegetable oil

4cm/1½in piece of fresh root ginger, sliced

4 garlic cloves, finely chopped

1 tsp Sichuan peppercorns

2 tsp dried chillies

2 tbsp Shaoxing rice wine

Dipping sauce

4 tbsp light soy sauce

2 garlic cloves, lightly crushed

1 red chilli, chopped

2 tbsp sesame oil

First make the dipping sauce: mix all the ingredients in a bowl and set aside to let the flavours infuse.

To cook the crayfish, fill a large saucepan with water and bring to the boil. Add the crayfish and cook for 2–3 minutes until the shells turn bright pink and the tails curve. Drain in a colander. Split them in half lengthwise, using a cleaver or large heavy knife, and discard the stomach sacs.

Heat a large wok over a medium–high heat, add the vegetable oil, then add the ginger, garlic, Sichuan peppercorns and dried chillies and stir-fry for 3 minutes. Add the boiled crayfish and toss well in the wok. Add the Shaoxing wine and cook for a further 1 minute. Serve immediately in a large bowl, with the dipping sauce on the side. These crayfish will be moist and tasty.

Lisa's tip If you can't get crayfish, this recipe also works well with raw king prawns in their shells, or even lobster for an indulgent meal.

SOFT-SHELL CRAB

SU ZHA RUAN KE XIE 酥炸软壳蟹

I first tasted this in Hong Kong; I was intrigued, as I had never known a crab without a hard shell. The chef told me that these were young crabs that had recently moulted their hard shell in order to grow, and were taken from the water before the new shell had hardened. So we could eat every part of the crab, including the legs. The beauty of soft-shell crab is that it's easy to eat but has all the depth and flavour of a normal crab. It was deep-fried in a light potato starch batter – the perfect way to enjoy this delicacy.

4 jumbo-sized soft-shell crabs,
  thawed if frozen

½ tsp salt

¼ tsp ground white pepper

1 egg, beaten in a shallow dish

4 tbsp potato starch

vegetable oil for deep-frying

1 spring onion (scallion), finely chopped

¼ onion, finely chopped

1 fresh red chilli, finely chopped

1 garlic clove, finely chopped

Seasoning

½ tsp salt

½ tsp sugar

½ tsp Chinese five-spice powder

Wash the crabs in cold water. Pat dry and sprinkle with salt and pepper. Dip the crabs in the beaten egg and then coat completely with potato starch.

Half-fill a wok or large saucepan with vegetable oil. Heat the oil to 180°C/350°F; if you don't have a cooking thermometer, test by dipping a wooden chopstick or wooden spoon into the oil – if bubbles immediately form around the chopstick the oil is hot enough. Deep-fry the coated crab for 5 minutes, carefully turning them over to cook on all sides. The crab legs will spread out as they cook and this will ensure the entire crab is crispy. Lift out with a slotted spoon and drain on paper towels.

Pour off the oil into a metal container. Put 1 tablespoon of the oil back into the wok over a high heat. Add the spring onion, onion, chilli and garlic and stir-fry for 1 minute. Add the cooked crab and season with salt, sugar and five-spice powder. Toss well and serve immediately.

Lisa's tip Soft-shell crab can be found in the freezer cabinets in Asian and Chinese grocery stores. Make sure you pick the jumbo size: the standard size crabs are tiny when cooked.

STIR-FRIED GLASS NOODLES

FEN SI 粉丝

The town of Zhangxing, near Zhaoyuan in Shangdong province, is famous for these noodles, made using the starch from mung beans, yams, potatoes or cassava. When cooked they are translucent like glass, hence the name (they are sometimes called cellophane noodles or bean threads). The white bundles of dried noodles look like rice vermicelli, but rice vermicelli remain white when cooked. They are naturally gluten free, and the locals like these noodles in soup because they are like sharks' fin – but cheaper and sustainable. The texture of glass noodles is quite slippery and gelatinous and they work well with seafood. When we were in the town, we had them in a variety of dishes, from braised Chinese mushrooms and tofu, to a soup with fish cake. This fish cake (sometimes called fish slice) is not the European-style fish cake with potatoes, but is a Chinese ingredient made from pounded fish; you can find it in the chiller cabinet of Chinese food shops.

6 tbsp vegetable oil

1 large onion, finely sliced

2 eggs, beaten

½ tsp finely chopped garlic

2cm/¾in piece of fresh root ginger, sliced

1 carrot, finely sliced

100g/3½oz kale, cut into strips

100g/3½oz pak choi, cut into thin strips

50g/1¾oz water chestnuts, sliced

100g/3½oz bean sprouts

100g/3½oz fish cake, cut into strips

3 nests of dried glass noodles, soaked in hot water for 5 minutes, drained and run under cold water

Flavourings

1 tbsp dark soy sauce

½ tsp salt

1 tsp caster (superfine) sugar

1 tsp sesame oil

1 tsp chilli bean paste

1 tsp Shaoxing rice wine

100ml/3½fl oz/scant ½ cup water

In a small bowl, mix all the flavourings together and set aside.

Heat a wok over a high heat, add 3 tablespoons of the vegetable oil, then add the onion and cook, stirring often, for 5–10 minutes, until brown and crisp. Drain on paper towels.

Put the wok back over a high heat and add 2 tablespoons of vegetable oil. When it starts to smoke, add the eggs, stir until scrambled, then turn out onto a plate and set aside.

In the same wok, add the remaining tablespoon of vegetable oil and stir-fry the garlic and ginger for a few seconds, then add the vegetables and fish cake and stir-fry for 5 minutes.

Finally, add the glass noodles and the flavourings and stir well. If the noodles are sticking together, use a wooden spoon or tongs to toss the noodles to ensure the flavourings are evenly dispersed. Add the scrambled eggs and mix well, then serve immediately, garnished with the crispy onions.

Lisa's tip Instead of the crispy onions you could garnish this dish with some crushed toasted cashew nuts.

SERVES 4
(MAKES 12)

PREP TIME
15 MINUTES
COOK TIME
8–10 MINUTES

TAKOYAKI BALLS

ZHANG YU SHAO 章魚燒

We visited Lantau Island (Hong Kong's largest island), where we saw a vendor making this version of a Japanese street food. *Takoyaki* balls are made from octopus which is cut into small pieces and mixed with herbs and spices in a batter, then poured into a special *takoyaki* pan and grilled. The *takoyaki* pan has hemispherical holes, and as the vendor skilfully turns the partly cooked batter, it almost miraculously becomes a golf-ball-like sphere. If you're using a muffin tin you won't get the same shape but these will still taste delicious. They are extremely light and this is an excellent way to cook octopus, which can sometimes be tough. My favourite takoyaki topping is dried bonito flakes and mayonnaise. Many supermarkets now sell Japanese ingredients; failing that, look for a specialist Asian retailer.

2 eggs

200g/7oz/generous 1½ cups plain (all-purpose) flour

200ml/7fl oz/generous ¾ cup dashi soup (dashi stock powder mixed with hot water)

500g/1lb 2oz boiled octopus, cut into small pieces

6 spring onions (scallions), finely chopped

100g/3½oz *beni shoga* (pickled red ginger), finely chopped

vegetable oil for greasing

Toppings

katsuobushi (dried bonito flakes)

aonori (green seaweed powder)

Worcestershire sauce or mayonnaise

Crack the eggs into a large bowl, add the flour and dashi soup and mix to a smooth batter. Add the octopus, spring onions and pickled ginger.

Preheat the grill to high. Grease the *takoyaki* pan or a 12-hole muffin tin. Pour in the batter and put under the grill for 3 minutes. Then flip the balls and cook on the other side for 3 minutes until golden brown. Remove the takoyaki from the moulds and serve with your choice of topping.

Lisa's tips Instead of pickled ginger, you could use finely chopped pickled vegetables.

If you make these in bigger moulds, they become octopus cupcakes – something different for a dinner party.

SICHUAN HOT AND SOUR SWEET POTATO NOODLES

SUAN LA FEN 酸辣粉

I watched the vendor peel the sweet potatoes and then, using a potato peeler, he spiralized the potato flesh, which was flash-boiled and then sautéed. It was then immersed in a spicy chilli broth mixed with seafood. I thought this was such a clever dish, using ingredients that were in abundance in Sichuan province and providing a great alternative to wheat noodles.

2 large sweet potatoes, peeled

2 tbsp vegetable oil

1 spring onion (scallion), finely chopped

200g/7oz white fish fillet,
    cut into small chunks

8–10 scallops

8–10 raw king prawns (shrimp),
    peeled and deveined

1 sprig of coriander (cilantro),
    finely chopped

3 tbsp Sichuan pickled vegetables,
    chopped, or 3 tbsp crushed peanuts,
    to garnish

Flavourings

1 garlic clove, finely chopped

½ tsp ground Sichuan peppercorns

½ tsp Chinese five-spice powder

1 tsp chilli oil

1 tbsp Chinese black vinegar

1 tbsp light soy sauce

½ tsp salt

Cut the sweet potatoes into thin strips, using a spiralizer if you have one. Alternatively, cut the potatoes into long, thin strips. Set aside.

In a small bowl, mix all the flavourings together and set aside.

Cook the sweet potato strips in a large saucepan of boiling water for 5 minutes, until softened. Drain and rinse in cold water.

Heat a wok over a high heat, add the vegetable oil, then add the the spring onion, fish and seafood and the coriander and stir-fry for about 3 minutes. When the seafood is fully cooked, add the cooked sweet potato and the flavourings. Mix well and toss for a further 3 minutes. Serve immediately, garnished with chopped pickled vegetables or crushed peanuts.

CHIVE AND PRAWN DUMPLINGS

JIU CAI JIAO 韭菜餃

These dumplings originate from Guangzhou and are a firm favourite in the dim sum tea houses. The chives lift these dumplings and give them a savoury fragrance. When steamed, the wrapper becomes translucent so you can see the beautiful pink colour of the prawns and the green of the chives. The wrapper is made with wheat starch, which you can buy from specialist Asian retailers. Dim sum means 'to touch your heart' and these dumplings are so beautiful that they will certainly touch your heart and also fill your stomach.

Wrappers

70g/2½oz/scant ½ cup tapioca flour, plus extra for dusting

125g/4½oz/1¼ cups wheat starch

½ tsp salt

180–200ml/6–7fl oz/about ¾ cup boiling water

2 tsp vegetable oil

sriracha hot chilli sauce or soy sauce, to serve

Filling

150g/5½oz raw peeled prawns (shrimp), very finely chopped

150g/5½oz chives, finely chopped

1 tbsp potato starch

½ tsp salt

pinch of ground white pepper

½ tbsp sesame oil

1 egg, beaten

To make the wrappers, mix the tapioca flour, wheat starch and salt in a bowl, then gradually add the boiling water and oil and mix to form a smooth dough. Cover the bowl with clingfilm and leave to rest for 15 minutes.

In another bowl, mix all the filling ingredients together.

Dust your work surface with tapioca flour and roll out the dough as thinly as possible. Use a pastry cutter or tumbler to cut out circles approx. 7cm/3in in diameter. Wet your index finger with water and moisten the outer rim of a wrapper. Place 1 heaped tablespoon of filling in the centre of the circle, fold over to form a half-moon shape and pleat the edges together. To do this, pinch the corner of the right-hand end of the dumpling. Using your index finger, crease one to two folds to the right to make a pleat. Continue to fold until the edge of the pastry is all pleated. Alternatively, use a fork to score a pattern along the edge. Repeat to make 12 dumplings.

To cook, either line a bamboo steamer basket with baking parchment or grease a plate with vegetable oil. Add the dumplings to the basket or plate, ensuring they do not touch. Put a trivet or round cake rack into a wok and add boiling water so it is just over a quarter full. Put the steamer basket or plate on top of the trivet, cover with a lid and steam for 10–15 minutes until the wrapper is translucent and the dumpling is firm to the touch. Serve hot with sriracha sauce or soy sauce.

Lisa's tip You can make extra and freeze the uncooked dumplings. When freezing, ensure they do not touch so they don't stick together. To serve, thaw, then steam for 15 minutes.

RAMEN IN SEAFOOD BROTH

HAI XIAN QING TANG MIAN 海鲜清汤拉面

Some people say that the Chinese invented noodles before the Italians. That debate could go on for a while, but ramen wheat noodles definitely originate from China, and were introduced to Japan at the beginning of the 20th century. Served in a broth with fish and prawns, the ramen absorbs the seafood flavours and is very tasty.

280g/10oz dried ramen noodles

3 tbsp vegetable oil

2cm/¾in piece of fresh root ginger,
    cut into thick slices

12 raw king prawns (shrimp), peeled
    and deveined

300g/10½oz white fish fillet,
    cut into 3cm/1¼in cubes

1 tsp salt

½ tsp ground white pepper

3 spring onions (scallions), sliced into
    2cm/¾in pieces

400ml/14fl oz/1⅔ cups seafood stock
    (see right)

2 tbsp soy sauce

1 tsp sesame oil

Fill a saucepan with just-boiled water and add the ramen. Do not heat, just let the ramen soak in the hot water for 2 minutes. Then drain so the ramen do not continue cooking. Set aside.

Put the same saucepan over a medium heat, add the vegetable oil and fry the ginger with the prawns and fish for about 4 minutes until the fish and prawns are just cooked. Add the salt, pepper and spring onions and fry for an additional 30 seconds. Add the stock and bring to the boil, then add the ramen, soy sauce and sesame oil and cook over a high heat for 1 minute. Serve immediately, in bowls.

Seafood Stock

Keep the shells and heads of any type of seafood, such as prawns or crayfish, as well as fish heads, to make a seafood stock. Put them in a saucepan or stockpot with a slice of ginger, a garlic clove, 1 small onion and 1 spring onion and add water to cover. Bring to the boil over a medium heat, then reduce the heat and simmer for 20 minutes. The liquid will reduce down by one-third. Strain into a bowl and leave to cool, then store in the fridge and use within 2 days or freeze for up to 3 months.

VEGETARIAN DISHES
素菜

MAKES APPROX.
10 ROLLS, DEPENDING
ON THE SIZE OF THE
BAKING TIN

PREP TIME
20 MINUTES
COOK TIME
5 MINUTES PER ROLL

RICE NOODLE ROLLS

CHANG FEN 腸粉

Chang fen are thin rice noodle sheets, which may be served plain or with a variety of fillings such as prawns, beef, or *char siu* (see page 18). I have not included a filling in this recipe, but I have indicated when it should be added in the method below. They are served in restaurants and by street vendors, often with a sprinkling of sesame seeds, chopped spring onions, soy sauce and plenty of peanut sauce or sriracha hot chilli sauce.

When my family and I returned to Guangzhou to rediscover our ancestral roots, we got off the train from Hong Kong to Guangzhou and a swarm of motorbikes surrounded us. They were actually taxis, but we didn't know that, and they persisted in hassling us. Dad decided to avoid the confrontation and ushered us all into a restaurant. My mum really wanted to eat *jie chang fen*, which literally translated means pigs' intestines, although there are no intestines in the dish; they are nicknamed that because at first glance the *chang fen* look like pigs' intestines. She called out to the waiter,

'Do you have any *jie chang fen*?'

The waiter sniggered and said, 'We've got the *jie* (indicating our mum), but not *chang fen*.'

We were all shocked at this rude response, so we upped and left. Mum was a bit despondent at the events of her first half hour in Guangzhou. Dad cheered her up. A few streets away, over a long, crumbling bridge, there was a nice little street café and they served *cheung fun*, so we sat there and ate. There were no fluorescent lights in this area and no hordes of motorbikes or traffic polluting the air. It was peaceful. However, as we sat in the open-front café, a storm cloud appeared, the heavens opened and sheets of rain poured down. Had we brought the rain from Manchester? Did bad things happen in threes? Mum shook her head, 'Sometimes you've just got to roll with the punches, kids. Now pass me the chilli sauce. I'm going to make my portion of *chang fen* extra spicy. I think I'm going to need the va va voom!'

200g/7oz/1¼ cups rice flour

2½ tbsp wheat starch

2½ tbsp potato starch or
cornflour (corn starch)

½ tsp salt

3 tbsp vegetable oil, plus extra for greasing

500ml/18fl oz/2 cups water

To serve

2 tbsp sesame seeds

2–3 spring onions (scallions), finely
chopped

soy sauce and other sauce(s) of your
choice, such as peanut sauce (page 56)
or sriracha hot chilli sauce

Put the flour, starches and salt into a large bowl. Pour in the oil and knead into the flour. Gradually add the water, a little at a time, and mix until it forms a thin batter.

You'll need a small rectangular or square non-stick baking tin, approx. 15 x 20cm/ 6 x 8in; grease the tin with oil and place it in a wok, then pour boiling water into the wok to come just below the level of the tin.

Pour about half a ladleful of the the batter into the baking tin to make a very thin layer and tilt to cover the surface and corners of the tin. If you want to add a filling, such as prawns or minced beef, chicken or pork, add them along the edge of one side of the batter. Put the tin of batter into the wok, cover the wok with a lid and steam for 5 minutes until the batter is opaque and set.

Grease a clean chopping board with oil. Using a plastic spatula, lift the layer of batter and roll up. Transfer the roll onto the chopping board and cut into 3cm/1¼in lengths. Repeat until you have used all the batter. To serve, place the rolls on a warmed serving plate and garnish with sesame seeds, spring onions and your choice of sauces.

Lisa's tip You can also make a sweet version, filled with tahini or grated white chocolate and sprinkled with black sesame seeds.

COLD NOODLE SALAD

MAJIANG LIANG PI 麻酱凉皮

The summer in Shanghai was scorching and I had lost my appetite. It was unthinkable to eat anything hot and meaty. My sister and I stumbled across a humble stall set back from all the hustle and bustle, selling cold noodles from a tricycle with a glass table precariously balanced on the handlebars. Initially I turned my nose up, thinking noodles had to be eaten hot. However, the popularity of the place convinced me otherwise and I gave them a go. When I bit into them, they were refreshing and packed with flavour – chilli, vinegar, salt, garlic, spring onions and cucumber – enhanced because of the cold temperature of the noodles.

4 tbsp vegetable oil

3 shallots, finely sliced

1 packet (500g) of Shanghai noodles
  or udon noodles

½ white cabbage, shredded

1 small carrot, cut into thin strips

100g/3½oz bean sprouts

¼ cucumber, deseeded and cut into
  long strips

1 spring onion (scallion), finely chopped

1 sprig of coriander (cilantro),
  finely chopped

Dressing

1 tbsp sesame oil

1 tsp chilli oil (optional)

½ tsp salt

½ tsp sugar

1 garlic clove, finely chopped

1 tbsp rice wine vinegar

1 tbsp light soy sauce

3 tbsp water

Heat a wok over a high heat, add 2 tablespoons of the vegetable oil, then add the shallots and cook, stirring often, for about 5 minutes, until brown and crispy. Drain on paper towels and set aside.

Bring a saucepan of water to the boil, turn off the heat, add the noodles and soak for 5 minutes. Drain and rinse in cold water. Drain well.

Put the wok back over a high heat, add the remaining vegetable oil and stir-fry the cabbage, carrot, bean sprouts, cucumber and spring onion for a few minutes. Add the drained noodles and coriander and mix well. Transfer to a large bowl and leave to cool.

To serve, add all the dressing ingredients and mix well. Serve garnished with the crispy shallots.

Lisa's tip Rice vermicelli are also good in this salad.

NOODLES IN SESAME PEANUT SAUCE

ZHĪMA MIÀN 芝麻面

On a hot summer night in Chengdu, I was deafened by the sound as a row of vendors were blending peanuts and sesame. I watched, fascinated, to see what they would do with this nutty sauce. They poured it onto noodles – a super-popular dish as the blenders were whizzing non-stop to satisfy the growing queues of hungry punters.

500g/1lb 2oz thin dried egg noodles

2 tbsp vegetable oil

1 onion, cut into thin wedges

1 turnip, cut into thin strips

50g/1¾oz mangetout (snow peas), sliced into thin strips

1 spring onion (scallion), finely chopped, to garnish

2 red chillies, finely chopped, to garnish

Seasonings

2 tbsp sesame paste

2 tbsp peanut butter

2 tbsp light soy sauce

½ tsp chilli oil

½ tsp salt

1 tbsp Shaoxing rice wine

½ tsp ground black pepper

½ tsp Thai fish sauce

150ml/5floz/⅔ cup water

Bring a saucepan of water to the boil, turn off the heat and put the noodles in the water to soak for 5 minutes. Drain and rinse in cold water to stop the cooking process. Drain.

Mix all the seasonings together and set aside.

Heat a wok over a high heat, add the vegetable oil and stir-fry the onion, turnip and mangetout for 4–5 minutes. Add the soaked noodles and then the seasonings. Toss well with tongs to ensure the seasonings are thoroughly mixed. Serve in bowls and garnish with chopped spring onions and chillies.

CHINESE LEAF WRAPS

SHŪCÀI BĀOGUǑ 蔬菜包裹

In China there are many temples; our tour guide took us to one near Xi'an, and we had 10 minutes to wander around before boarding the coach. I noticed a queue of people lined up at a food cart so I went to have a peek. The young man was skilfully and speedily rolling Chinese leaves, and as I got closer he stir-fried a colourful array of vegetables and then used them to fill the leaves. I queued up for one of these wraps and had to run for the bus, but I made it and sat down to enjoy my wonderful veggie surprise.

1 head of Chinese leaf (napa cabbage)

100g/3½oz bamboo shoots, diced

100g/3½oz water chestnuts, diced

1 celery stick, diced

100g/3½oz dried Chinese mushrooms, soaked in hot water for 20 minutes, then cut into small dice

100g/3½oz mangetout (snow peas), sliced

100g/3½oz sweetcorn kernels

2 tbsp vegetable oil

2cm/¾in piece of fresh root ginger, finely chopped

1 tsp salt

1 tsp sugar

½ tsp Chinese five-spice powder

1 tsp sesame oil

1 tsp Shaoxing rice wine

150ml/5floz/⅔ cup water

1 tbsp potato starch mixed with 2 tbsp cold water

hoisin sauce, for dipping

Separate the leaves from the head of Chinese leaf and set aside.

Prepare all the vegetables and place in a bowl ready to cook. Heat a wok over a high heat, add the vegetable oil, then add the ginger and all the diced vegetables and season with the salt, sugar, five-spice powder, sesame oil and wine and stir-fry for 4–5 minutes. Add the water and then blend in the potato starch mixture to thicken. Leave to cool.

Put the Chinese leaves into a bowl and pour over freshly boiled water to cover them; leave until just wilted, then remove from the water and rinse in cold water to stop the cooking process. Drain on paper towels and leave to cool.

Put 1 tablespoon of the vegetable mixture onto the edge of each leaf. Roll the leaf forward, folding in the sides to make a parcel. Repeat until all the leaves and mixture have been used up.

Serve with hoisin sauce for dipping.

MA PO TOFU WITH AUBERGINES

MA PO DOU FU QIE ZI 麻婆豆付茄子

Down the road from our hotel in Sichuan there was a busy night market and I could see the smoke billowing from a food cart. As I approached, the vendor was enveloped in smoke and all you could see was his silhouette. The smell of aubergines and chillies made me hungry, so I called out '*yi ge*,' meaning one please. This spicy, sour and earthy dish is one of the best dishes I have tasted for only 10 yuan. Bargain!

4 x 100g/3½oz blocks of firm tofu

2 aubergines (eggplants)

2 tbsp vegetable oil

1 onion, diced

3 garlic cloves, finely chopped

1 tbsp chilli bean paste

350ml/12fl oz/1½ cups vegetable stock

1 tsp salt

½ tsp ground black pepper

1 tbsp light soy sauce

1 tbsp Shaoxing rice wine

1 tsp sesame oil

1 tsp chilli oil

2 tsp potato starch mixed
with 1 tbsp water

2 spring onions (scallions),
finely sliced, to garnish

Drain the tofu, pat dry and cut into 1cm/½in cubes. Leaving the skin on the aubergines, cut them into 2cm/¾in cubes. Set aside.

Heat a wok over a high heat, add the vegetable oil and stir-fry the onion, garlic and aubergines with the chilli bean paste for 2–3 minutes. Add the stock and cook for a further 5 minutes.

Add the tofu cubes to the wok and season with the salt, pepper, soy sauce, wine, sesame oil and chilli oil. Add the potato starch mixture and stir briefly over a high heat until the mixture thickens. Serve at once, garnished with spring onions.

Lisa's tip Take care to stir gently after adding the tofu, to avoid it crumbling.

CAULIFLOWER, LEEK AND RED PEPPER SKEWERS

KAO SHU CAI 烤蔬菜

At the night market, trays of skewered vegetables were piled high. The smell of charred leeks and chillies lingered in the air. The vendor was mopping oil over the vegetable skewers and next to him was an array of pots with dried spices, condiments and seasonings. We had to try one of these skewers; the flavours were a delicious blend of spicy, sweet and salty.

1 large cauliflower

1 large leek, washed thoroughly

2 large red peppers

8 large red chillies, stems removed

3 tbsp vegetable oil

1 tsp salt

pinch of ground white pepper

pinch of Chinese five-spice powder

sweet chilli sauce, to serve

Soak 8 wooden skewers in water for 25 minutes.

While the skewers are soaking, cut the cauliflower into florets, chop the leek into thick slices and cut the peppers into squares; all the pieces should be of a similar size.

Mix the oil, salt, pepper and five-spice powder in a large bowl, add the prepared vegetables and the chillies and toss to ensure each piece is evenly coated with the oil. Thread the vegetables onto the skewers.

Heat a griddle pan until it is very hot. Place the skewers on the griddle and cook for about 4–5 minutes on each side until charred. Serve hot, with sweet chilli sauce.

Lisa's tip This simple dish showcases the freshness of the vegetables. Mushrooms, asparagus or broccoli would also work well in this recipe.

SERVES 4

PREP TIME
3 WEEKS TO MAKE THE
BRINE, 3 HOURS TO
MARINATE THE TOFU
COOK TIME
5 MINUTES

STINKY TOFU

CHOU DOU FU 臭豆腐

'What the heck is that smell?' screeched my sister, holding her nose. 'It stinks to high heaven!'

Then we saw the stinky tofu vendor with wafts of smoke billowing out around him. 'You gotta try this stuff. Come on, get it down you!' I retorted.

'Not unless you try it too.'

So we hesitantly edged towards the stinky tofu man and ordered one portion to share between us. The locals giggled at us looking so sheepish and then making a big song and dance as we ate the tofu.

Tastewise it was actually OK. The tofu is 'fermented' in brine and that is what makes it smell. Without that fermentation tofu is generally very bland. This recipe is our take on the stinky tofu – after all, we don't want you to get into trouble with Environmental Health and your neighbours.

400g/14oz firm tofu, cut into 5–6cm/
   2–2½in slices

2 tbsp vegetable oil

2 tbsp Chinese black vinegar

½ tsp chilli paste

2 tbsp soy sauce

Brine
2 litres/3½ pints/8 cups soya milk

50g/1¾oz/4 tbsp sugar

1 tbsp salt

1 tbsp vanilla extract

First make the brine: put all the ingredients into a clean, sterilized bucket with a lid. It will initially look white. Leave for 3 weeks until it looks mouldy grey (this is part of the fermentation process). That's the brine ready.

Place the tofu pieces in the brine for 3 hours. Lift out with a slotted spoon and drain on paper towels. The tofu is now ready to fry. Beware – it will smell very pungent.

Heat a wok over a high heat, add the oil, then add the tofu and cook for 2 minutes on each side until crispy. This will create quite a stench in the kitchen, but like cheese connoisseurs, if you can get past the smell, you are in for a treat. Now add the black vinegar, chilli paste and soy sauce. Mix thoroughly and serve.

Lisa's tip You can simply use firm tofu if you don't want to stink out your kitchen and incur the wrath of the neighbours!

SERVES 4

PREP TIME
30 MINUTES, PLUS
2 HOURS RESTING
COOK TIME
10 MINUTES

FRIED DOUGH STICKS

YOU TIAO 油條

I remember in Hong Kong having *you tiao* with our congee (rice porridge). It consists of two pieces of dough joined together side by side, and as kids we loved them. Mum used to buy us one to share and we'd tear it down the middle and like magic there were two deliciously crunchy *you tiao* – one each, so no fighting! They were crunchy on the outside and chewy on the inside – a perfect contrast in texture to the porridge-like congee. We nicknamed them Chinese-style doughnuts, but they're salty to taste, not sweet.

1 tbsp baking powder

½ tsp salt

200ml/7fl oz/generous ¾ cup water

300g/10½oz/scant 2½ cups plain (all-purpose) flour, plus extra for dusting

3 tbsp vegetable oil, plus extra for deep-frying

In a bowl mix the baking powder, salt and water until dissolved. Sift the flour into the bowl and mix until it forms a sticky dough. Leave to rest for 20 minutes.

Fold and knead the dough until it feels elastic. Shape into a ball and place in a bowl, cover with the vegetable oil, cover the bowl with clingfilm and leave in a warm place for 1½ hours.

Turn the dough onto a floured work surface and use a rolling pin to roll into a long rectangle, about 20 x 30cm/8 x 12in. Fold the dough over from top to bottom and cut into double-layered strips approx. 2cm/¾in wide. Use a chopstick to imprint a groove along the centre of each strip. Stretch them out slightly by pulling on both ends. They will spring back as they cook.

Half-fill a wok with vegetable oil. Heat the oil to 180°C/350°F; if you don't have a cooking thermometer, test by dipping a wooden chopstick or wooden spoon into the oil – if bubbles immediately form around the chopstick the oil is hot enough. Gently place the dough strips into the oil. Cook for 3–4 minutes on each side until golden brown. Cook in batches to prevent the oil dropping in temperature. Drain on paper towels. Serve warm.

Lisa's tip If you want a richer taste, replace the water with milk; warm the milk in the microwave before adding to the dough mixture.

SOUR AND SPICY SHREDDED POTATO

SUAN LA TU DOU SI 酸辣土豆丝

Abby, our tour guide in Beijing, asked us if we were hungry. Oh yes, we were. So she led us to a narrow street where a vendor was selling these amazing *toudou si*. She explained that the inspiration for this dish came from the Spanish empire, many centuries ago. Potatoes thrive in the area around Beijing due to the dry climate and cold winters. The combination of potatoes and chillies, although simple, was filling and delicious. It sure beats a bag of chips from the chip shop.

2 large potatoes, peeled and
   finely shredded

2 tbsp vegetable oil

2 garlic cloves, finely chopped

2 fresh chillies, finely sliced

25g/1oz sour pickled mustard greens,
   finely diced

1 tsp salt

1 tsp sugar

1 tsp chilli oil

1 tsp light soy sauce

1 tsp sesame oil

2 tbsp water

Cook the potatoes in a saucepan of boiling water for 2–3 minutes, then drain.

Heat a wok over a high heat, add the vegetable oil and stir-fry the garlic, chillies and sour pickles for 2–3 minutes. Add the potatoes and toss well. Add the salt, sugar, chilli oil, soy sauce, sesame oil and water. Toss well with tongs to ensure the seasonings are thoroughly mixed. Serve hot.

Lisa's tip Pickled mustard greens are available from Asian food stores, but if you can't find them you can substitute pickled gherkins.

SPIRAL POTATO CHIPS

LUO XUAN SHU TIAO 螺旋薯條

We saw these on many street food vendors' carts. Not only are they beautiful to look at but they are also quite delicious. If you don't have a spiralizer, we've explained how to cut the potato to create a similar effect.

8 small potatoes, peeled
vegetable oil for deep-frying
pinch of salt and pepper
Sweet Mandarin Wasabi Sauce,
    to serve

Cut a small slice off one end of a potato. Insert a bamboo skewer through the middle of the cut end, all the way to the other end of the potato.

Holding a small, sharp knife at a slight angle, carefully slice the potato in a clockwise motion while turning it in an anticlockwise direction (or opposite if you are left-handed). Separate out the potato to create the spiral.

Half-fill a wok or large saucepan with vegetable oil. Heat the oil to 180°C/350°F; if you don't have a cooking thermometer, test by dipping a wooden chopstick or wooden spoon into the oil – if bubbles immediately form around the chopstick the oil is hot enough. Deep-fry the potato spirals for 6–8 minutes until crisp and fully cooked. Cook in batches to prevent the oil dropping in temperature. Drain on paper towels and sprinkle with salt and pepper. Serve with wasabi sauce.

Lisa's tip Choose small potatoes so you don't need as much oil to fry them.

SWEET POTATO

HONG SHU 紅薯

I've learnt never to haggle with a street vendor in Beijing unless you intend to buy. To ask 'How much?' is essentially committing to the deal – which I learnt the hard way when I asked a sweet potato seller how much was one sweet potato. The air was freezing and we'd just finished traipsing around the Forbidden City. He immediately threw about six sweet potatoes into a bag and put out his hand to receive the money – 30 yuan! I said I only wanted one but he was adamant on selling me the entire bag. So I walked off. The vendor followed me down the street, swinging a boiling hot bag of freshly steamed sweet potatoes and at one point almost hitting my head in his enthusiasm. I began to run. He chased me down, leaving his cart – and probably his day's takings – unattended, just to get me to buy this bag of sweet potatoes. I was horrified and ran as fast as I could. I jumped over a parked bike which fell into his path and stopped him in his tracks. He gave up the chase. I could still hear him shouting at me angrily. I didn't look back and just kept running. I only wanted one sweet potato as a snack. When I make this dish, I can now chuckle at this memory.

4 large sweet potatoes, peeled

3 tbsp vegetable oil

1 tsp salt

½ tsp Chinese five-spice powder

Preheat the oven to 200°C/400°F/gas 6.

Cook the sweet potatoes in a large saucepan of boiling water for 20 minutes until completely soft. Drain and pat dry.

Coat in the vegetable oil and place on a non-stick baking dish. Sprinkle with the salt and five-spice powder and bake in the oven for about 15 minutes. Serve hot.

Lisa's tip Instead of boiling and baking, you can slice the peeled sweet potatoes very thinly and then deep-fry them in a wok of hot oil for 2–3 minutes to make sweet potato crisps.

OIL-FRIED RICE CAKES

YOU ZI 油糍

If you ever get the chance to go to Jiujiang, visit Stone Bell Hill, where you can try these oil-fried rice cakes. The clash of the red chillies and the green chives apparently symbolize the place, visible from the hill, where the Yangtze River and the waters of Boyang Lake converge with an abrupt colour change. Over the centuries, visitors have been intrigued by the 'stone bell' sound resonating from the cliffs overlooking this spot and have put forward various theories about this rare geographical phenomenon. Chinese artists have left more than twenty calligraphy masterpieces carved upon its rocks, with some dating back to the Tang dynasty (618–907).

100ml/3½fl oz/scant ½ cup cold water

1 tsp salt

1 onion, finely sliced

1 tsp finely chopped garlic

1 red chilli, finely chopped

2 chives, finely chopped

80g/just under 3oz/scant ¾ cup plain (all-purpose) flour, sifted, plus extra for dusting

80g/just under 3oz/½ cup glutinous rice flour, sifted

vegetable oil for deep-frying

Put the water into a saucepan, add the salt, onion, garlic, chilli and chives and cook for 5 minutes until bubbling. Add both flours and mix to a stiff dough. Cover with a lid and leave to steam over a low heat for 15 minutes.

Scoop out the mixture onto a floured work surface; at first the texture will be like breadcrumbs. Knead the mixture for 15 minutes to form a smooth dough. Divide the dough into two equal pieces. Using a rolling pin, roll out the dough into large rectangles, about 1cm/½in thick. Using a 5–6cm/2–2½in diameter pastry cutter, cut out circles of dough until you have used all the dough.

Half-fill a wok or large saucepan with vegetable oil. Heat the oil to 180°C/350°F; if you don't have a cooking thermometer, test by dipping a wooden chopstick or wooden spoon into the oil – if bubbles immediately form around the chopstick the oil is hot enough.

Place four or five dough circles into the hot oil and turn over continuously while cooking. After 4–5 minutes the cakes will turn golden brown. Using a slotted spoon, lift them out, drain on paper towels and keep them warm while you cook the remaining dough. Serve hot.

Lisa's tip To add colour, add ½ teaspoon ground turmeric with the onion and garlic at the beginning of the recipe.

**SERVES 4–8
(MAKES 16)**

PREP TIME
30 MINUTES, PLUS
30 MINUTES RESTING
COOK TIME
15 MINUTES

SPRING ONION PANCAKES

CONG YOU BING 蔥油餅

This is a great combination of flavours that just is so satisfying and moreish. I like to serve it with XO sauce (a spicy seafood sauce from Hong Kong) to give it some spicy seafood flavour – but then it's no longer vegetarian.

This dish also has a story – though it's more fable than fact. The Xinhua newspaper reported that the spring onion pancake was the humble beginning of the pizza. Apparently, Marco Polo had fallen in love with this dish in China and wanted to introduce it to Italy. Italian chefs struggled to put the filling in the middle of the pancake, so they ended up putting the filling on top of the dough and adding a bit of cheese along the way – hence creating the pizza! Unfortunately for this story, historical evidence suggests that pizza existed in the Mediterranean long before Marco Polo's time. The first recorded use of the word 'pizza' dates from 997AD (in a Latin text from southern Italy), more than 250 years before Marco Polo was born. Nonetheless, I thought I would share the story with you.

400g/14oz/3¼ cups cups plain
(all-purpose) flour, plus extra for dusting

1 tsp salt

220ml/8floz/scant 1 cup cold water

4 tbsp warm water

9 tbsp vegetable oil

6 spring onions (scallions), chopped

Sift the flour and salt into a bowl and gradually add the cold water, mixing to make a sticky dough. Add the warm water and knead the dough until smooth. Place in a bowl, cover with a damp tea towel and leave to rest for 30 minutes.

Mix 6 tablespoons of the vegetable oil with the spring onions and set aside.

Turn out the dough onto a lightly floured work surface and knead lightly, then divide it into four equal pieces. Roll out each piece into a rectangle about 20 x 10cm/8 x 4in. Spoon 1 heaped tablespoon of the spring onion mixture onto each piece of dough and spread it to cover the dough.

Starting at one of the long sides, gently roll up each piece of dough to make a log shape. Coil each log into a snail shape and tuck the end underneath. Using the rolling pin, roll out the dough into a pancake about 5mm/¼in thick; try not to break the dough when rolling out: if it is a bit thicker, just cook it for slightly longer.

Heat a frying pan over a medium–high heat and add the remaining 3 tablespoons of oil. Cook the pancakes one at a time for about 1–2 minutes on each side. Keep the pancakes warm while you cook the rest of the batch, then serve hot.

Lisa's tip To make these spicier, add a drop or two of chilli oil to the spring onion mixture.

SERVES 4

PREP TIME
1 HOUR, PLUS
2 HOURS RESTING
COOK TIME
15–20 MINUTES

XI'AN NAN BREAD

NANG 馕

Walking around the streets of Xi'an we saw tables covered with tablecloths and these large golden discs of bread, looking like rows and rows of massive bagels. From a distance the golden colour was so distinctive that I had to go and inspect them further. I bought one and immediately tore off a piece of this thick dry *nang*. It was dense and chewy like a bagel. In a nearby café I saw people eating the bread dipped in tea. I smiled, thinking about how I prefer the Western-style tea and biscuits, but this bread would go well with soup or any saucy dish.

335ml/11½fl oz/scant1½ cups warm
   water

2 tsp dried yeast

500g/1lb 2oz/4 cups plain (all-purpose)
   flour, plus extra for dusting

2 tsp salt

1 tsp sugar

1 egg, beaten

2 tsp cumin seeds or sesame seeds

vegetable oil for brushing

Mix the water and yeast in a small bowl and leave for 5 minutes until frothy.

Sift the flour into a large bowl, add the salt, sugar and beaten egg and mix. Gradually add the yeast water and mix until it forms a dough. Knead for 10–15 minutes until smooth. Shape the dough into a ball, brush lightly with vegetable oil, place in a bowl and cover with a damp tea towel; leave to rest in a warm place for 2 hours.

Preheat the oven to 200°/400°F/gas 6.

Turn the dough out onto a lightly floured work surface, knead lightly, then divide the dough into four or five balls. Roll each dough ball into a 13cm/5in diameter disc. Raise the dough all around the circumference of the disc and tuck the dough back in on itself to form a raised edge all around. Using a small pastry cutter or other round shape, press gently into the dough to mark round patterns in the centre, then use a fork to mark holes all over the dough. Brush all over with vegetable oil, then sprinkle with cumin or sesame seeds. Bake for 15 minutes, or until golden.

MAKES 15 SPRING
ROLLS

PREP TIME
20 MINUTES
COOK TIME
30 MINUTES

VEGETARIAN SPRING ROLLS

CHUN JUAN 春捲

One Chinese New Year, I remember my dad drinking too many beers and ending up waving about ten spring rolls in each hand, shouting 'I'm going to get rich this year! Look how many gold bars I've got.' This was a time before there were such things as the lottery. We were laughing so hard that we had tears running down our faces. Dad never got rich that year but our New Year certainly started with a bang. Spring rolls resemble gold bars and symbolize wealth, and are particularly popular during Chinese New Year. They come with a variety of fillings. Dad likes vegetable. Mum likes chicken. Such is life.

2 tbsp vegetable oil, plus extra for
    deep-frying

250g/9oz bean sprouts

10 dried Chinese mushrooms, soaked in
    hot water for 20 minutes, then drained
    and finely sliced

50g/1¾oz carrots, finely sliced, blanched

50g/1¾oz bamboo shoots, finely sliced

50g/1¾oz glass vermicelli noodles
    (bean threads), soaked in hot water
    for 5 minutes, then drained

pinch of salt

pinch of sugar

pinch of Chinese five-spice powder

drop of sesame oil

2 tsp light soy sauce

15 spring roll wrappers

1 tbsp plain (all-purpose) flour and
    2 tbsp water, mixed to make a paste

sweet chilli sauce, to serve

Heat the wok over a high heat and add 1 tablespoon of the vegetable oil. Add the bean sprouts, mushrooms, carrots, bamboo shoots and noodles, season with the salt, sugar, five-spice powder, sesame oil and soy sauce and stir-fry for 5 minutes, then set aside. Tip the mixture into a colander to drain off any excess liquid.

Separate the spring roll wrappers. Put the first wrapper on a clean work surface at an angle, so the point of a diamond shape is nearest you. Place 1 tablespoon of the filling near the point of the wrapper and roll it forward. When the wrapper is rolled halfway, fold in the sides on the left and right. Brush some of the flour paste on the top corner and roll forward to close the spring roll. Continue until you have made all the spring rolls. *Illustrated overleaf.*

Half-fill a wok or saucepan with vegetable oil. Heat the oil to 180°C/350°F; if you don't have a cooking thermometer, test by dipping a wooden chopstick or wooden spoon into the oil – if bubbles immediately form around the chopstick the oil is hot enough. Carefully drop in three or four spring rolls and cook for 6–7 minutes, turning occasionally, until golden brown on both sides. (Cook in batches to prevent the oil from dropping in temperature.) Drain on paper towels. Serve hot with sweet chilli sauce for dipping.

Lisa's tips The uncooked spring rolls can be frozen for up to one month in a well-sealed airtight container. Thaw and deep-fry from frozen, in batches.

SERVES 4

PREP TIME
10 MINUTES, PLUS
8 HOURS BRINING
COOK TIME
0 MINUTES

HUNAN PICKLES

HÚNÁN PÀOCÀI 湖南泡菜

Pickling and fermentation is an art in Hunan province. We often saw these pickles brined in huge glass jars with long ladles ready to scoop out a portion to go or to eat there and then. The sourness hits your nasal passages when they scoop it out and the taste of these pickles is sharp and tangy: these are a must-try.

300g/10½oz white cabbage, chopped into small cubes

1 carrot, sliced into diamond shapes

1 small cucumber, sliced into rounds

4 small red chillies

5cm/2in piece of fresh root ginger

3 whole garlic cloves

10 Sichuan peppercorns

100ml/3½fl oz/scant ½ cup sorghum wine

300ml/10fl oz/1¼ cups white vinegar

1 tsp salt

500ml/18fl oz/2 cups water

Dry the vegetables on paper towels. Put all the ingredients in a large sterilized glass jar and leave for at least 8 hours.

The pickles will keep for several months.

Lisa's tip Sorghum wine, also known as *baijiu*, is available from Asian or Chinese retailers.

STEAMED YAM CAKE

ZHENG YU TOU GAO 蒸芋頭羔

MAKES 4

PREP TIME
20 MINUTES
COOK TIME
50 MINUTES

We had a reunion with one of my old corporate lawyer friends in Hong Kong and being a foodie I really wanted to try the steamed yam cake. So she took us to a little stall where these were freshly made. On the stall there were three people working a production line: one peeling the yams and chopping, one mixing and filling the tins and one serving the customers. The one serving would lift up a massive bamboo lid and lift out one of the yam cakes, then slice it on a wooden board. He scooped them up and served them on a long tray with a fork. We asked for three forks and sat on some steps, grabbing bites of freshly made yam cake and catching up on the good old days.

3 tbsp vegetable oil

3 shallots, finely sliced

500g/1lb 2oz yam or taro, peeled and
cut into small dice

50g/1¾oz dried Chinese mushrooms,
soaked in hot water for 20 minutes,
drained, then cut into small dice

1 tsp salt

¼ tsp Chinese five-spice powder

1 tsp sugar

2 tbsp light soy sauce

200g/7oz/1¼ cups rice flour

250ml/9fl oz/1 cup water

450ml/16fl oz/generous 1¾ cups
vegetable stock (this can include the
water from soaking the dried mushrooms)

2 spring onions (scallions), finely chopped

1 sprig of coriander (cilantro),
finely chopped

Line a 23cm/9in loaf tin with baking parchment.

Heat a wok over a high heat, add 2 tablespoons of the vegetable oil and stir-fry the shallots for about 5 minutes until they are crispy. Scoop out with a slotted spoon and drain on paper towels. Set aside.

In the same wok, add the remaining oil and stir-fry the yam and mushrooms for 5–6 minutes until softened. Season with the salt, five-spice powder, sugar and soy sauce and mix well.

In a bowl, mix the rice flour and water until blended. Add the stock and stir well, then add the cooked yam, mushrooms and shallots and stir again. Pour the mixture into the loaf tin. Bang the tin on the work surface to remove any air bubbles and ensure the mixture is evenly distributed.

Half-fill a wok with hot water and put a trivet or round cake rack in the wok. Put the loaf tin on the trivet, cover the wok with a lid and steam over a high heat for 40 minutes.

Slice the steamed yam cake into 1.5cm/⅝in thick slices and serve warm, sprinkled with spring onions and coriander.

VEGETABLE OMELETTE

DAN BING 蛋餅

I saw trays and trays of eggs in the market stall. Behind it were cages of hens making a din. The stallholder in his string vest was like a conductor at his wok. He cracked the eggs into a container and beat them with his wooden chopsticks, then he fired up the wok and a burst of smoke shot upwards before he created a spectacular omelette. He was calling out as loudly as he could, 'Egg pancakes. Come and get them while they are hot.' I watched as visitors were drawn from left to right until finally it was my turn to get one of these soft and fluffy omelettes.

2 tbsp vegetable oil

1 onion, finely sliced

100g/3½oz green beans, sliced

8 large eggs, beaten

½ tsp salt

pinch of ground white pepper

Heat the wok over a medium heat and add the oil. Add the onion and fry until translucent, then add the green beans and fry for a further 3 minutes.

Season the eggs with the salt and pepper, then add the eggs to the wok and swirl to spread them as thinly as possible so they cook evenly. Once one side has set – about 3 minutes – flip and cook the other side for 2 minutes. Roll the omelette up, cut into four portions and serve hot.

Lisa's tip This is great for breakfast.

QUAILS' EGGS

AN CHUN DAN 鵪鶉蛋

Quails' eggs are considered a delicacy in many parts of the world. They are much smaller than hens' eggs: about four quails' eggs are equivalent to one hen's egg. But they have a big yolk relative to the amount of white, a richer flavour and a more delicate texture.

I was fascinated by a particular street vendor in Shenzen who was selling what looked like miniature tangerines. On closer inspection they were quails' eggs dipped in an orange-coloured batter and deep-fried, then skewered for ease of eating on the go. What was wonderful was that they were soft boiled and the different textures – the oozy yolk, the smooth white and the crisp batter – made an exciting combination and turned a simple egg into a street-food delicacy.

12 quails' eggs

100g/3½oz/1 cup panko breadcrumbs

1 tsp salt

¼ tsp Chinese five-spice powder

pinch of red chilli powder

1 large hen's egg, beaten

vegetable oil for deep-frying

sweet chilli sauce or sriracha hot chilli sauce, to serve

Lower the quails' eggs into a pan of boiling water and boil for 2 minutes. Drain the eggs and run them under cold water to stop the cooking process. Peel the eggs.

Place the panko crumbs on a plate and add the salt, five-spice powder and chilli powder. Mix thoroughly. Dip the peeled quails' eggs into the beaten egg and then dip them into the panko crumbs, gently turning them until they are fully coated.

Half-fill a saucepan with vegetable oil. Heat the oil to 180°C/350°F; if you don't have a cooking thermometer, test by dipping a wooden chopstick or wooden spoon into the oil – if bubbles immediately form around the chopstick the oil is hot enough. Turn the heat down to medium. Put all the quails' eggs into the hot oil and cook for 45 seconds. Lift out with a slotted spoon and drain on paper towels. Serve with sweet chilli sauce or sriracha sauce.

Lisa's tip These eggs can also be served hard boiled if you don't want a runny egg – boil for 4 minutes instead of 2.

TEA EGGS
CHA YE DAN 茶叶蛋

MAKES 8

PREP TIME
10 MINUTES, PLUS
5 HOURS SOAKING
COOK TIME
1 HOUR

In Zhelaizhai, on the fringes of the Gobi Desert in north-west China, the majority of the villagers have piercing blue or green eyes, some have long noses, some even have fair hair. DNA tests prove that these features are Caucasian in origin and it is thought that the villagers are descended from a lost legion of Roman soldiers, many generations ago.

While the archaeologists conducted digs in the region, along the ancient Silk Route, something closer to home caught my attention: tea eggs. The family with whom I was staying had gone to work in the fields and they said that they wouldn't be back until dark. I looked forward to exploring the area. I thought I would fit in, being ethnically Chinese, but I stood out like a sore thumb. As I wandered around the village, some villagers were washing in the nearby lake, others were huddled under the trees – some of them were cooking.

A deeply wrinkled woman with emerald eyes caught my attention. With five or six young children all tugging at her dress she waved me over and offered me a tea egg from a pot of black liquid containing various spices and tea. The smell was intoxicating and made my stomach grumble. As we spoke different languages we had to communicate with lots of smiling and hand gestures.

The egg was beautifully marbled, where the spice and tea mixture permeated the cracked shell. The scent was earthy, slightly salty, with a subtle spice. The yolk had a thin, greyish layer and a yellow centre and the tea brought out the yolk's flavour. As I set off again the kids took a liking to my shiny shoes and started to dance around me, their laughter echoing across the village.

8 eggs

200ml/7fl oz/generous ¾ cup dark soy sauce

3 star anise

3 tbsp black (oolong) leaf tea

1 cinnamon stick

1 tsp brown sugar

1 tbsp Chinese five-spice powder

2 strips of dried tangerine or mandarin orange peel

Boil the eggs in a saucepan for 5 minutes, then lift them out using a slotted spoon and cool under cold water. Crack the eggshells all over.

Put the eggs back into the pan of hot water, add the remaining ingredients and simmer for 30 minutes over a low heat.

Turn off the heat and leave the eggs in the liquid for at least 5 hours – preferably overnight.

Serve cold or warm.

Lisa's tip These would make a wonderful breakfast – especially at Easter. They are also great cut into quarters and served on a bowl of steaming hot noodles.

CHINESE CRÊPES

JIĀNBING 中國煎餅

When we visited China, every morning the road would come alive with vendors selling these Chinese crêpes. After breakfast time, or when they had finished selling their wares, they'd pack up and go to the next foodie street, restock their ingredients and prepare to cook and serve lunch. It was fascinating to see them at work – skilfully tossing the pancakes and filling them with a variety of fillings, such as egg, herbs and chilli sauce to make savoury *jianbing*; another vendor might fill them with banana, cream and chocolate sauce. Here is the basic recipe; you can add whatever filling you want, such as chopped bacon, beef, pork or chicken.

5 tbsp millet flour

5 tbsp plain (all-purpose) flour

200ml/7fl oz/generous ¾ cup soya milk

½ tsp salt

1 tbsp vegetable oil, plus extra for frying

Filling

4 eggs

2 spring onions (scallions), finely chopped

pinch of salt and pepper

sriracha hot chilli sauce, to serve (optional)

In a bowl combine both flours, the soya milk, salt and vegetable oil to make a smooth batter.

Heat a wok or non-stick frying pan over a medium–high heat and add about 2 tablespoons of vegetable oil, swirling it around to ensure the wok is coated with oil. When hot, add a quarter of the batter and swirl to coat the wok with a thin layer of batter. Cook for 1 minute. Flip over and cook the other side for 1 minute.

Crack an egg onto the pancake and swirl it around until it's cooked to your liking. Add a sprinkling of spring onions and a pinch of salt and pepper. If you like, add some sriracha sauce for added spicy heat.

Fold the left side of the pancake to the middle, then fold in the right side so the pancake becomes a cylindrical roll. Repeat to make four pancakes and serve hot.

DESSERTS
甜点

EIGHT TREASURES CAKE

JING GAO 镜糕

When we visited Suzhou, about 100km (60 miles) north-west of Shanghai, this dessert was sold on every street corner. One vendor was singing his heart out to attract business and it caught my attention because his voice was like an opera singer's and it didn't quite match his biker jacket look. We tried his eight treasures cake, which was solid and dense. Every mouthful had different 'treasures' and it was super-sweet. It was quite different from any dessert I had ever tasted and I asked the vendor how he made it. He sang back, 'I'll show you.' And he smiled from ear to ear as he sang out the ingredients and steps. We laughed so much that we had to include the recipe in this book – it brings back such a happy memory.

125g/4½oz/⅔ cup glutinous rice

200ml/7fl oz/generous ¾ cup cold water

25g/1oz dried pineapple, roughly sliced into small pieces

25g/1oz dried cherries, roughly diced into small pieces

25g/1oz dried mango, roughly diced into small pieces

25g/1oz dried apricots, roughly diced into small pieces

25g/1oz dried coconut flakes

25g/1oz cashew nuts, roughly diced into small pieces

25g/1oz raisins

70g/2½oz red bean paste

vegetable oil for greasing

Rinse the rice with cold water three times and drain. Then add the measured water to the rice and cook in a saucepan or a rice cooker until the rice is fully cooked and the grains are fluffy.

Scoop the rice into a bowl. Add most of the dried fruit, nuts, raisins and red bean paste and mix thoroughly. (Reserve some of the fruit and nuts for decoration.)

Grease four or six ramekins with vegetable oil and fill them with the rice mixture, pushing the mixture down so there are no gaps. Decorate the tops with dried fruit and nuts. Place a trivet or round cake rack in a wok and fill the wok halfway with boiling water (alternatively use a steamer basket). Sit the ramekins on the rack, cover and steam for 45 minutes. Serve hot or warm.

Lisa's tip These can be made in advance and reheated by steaming for 15 minutes when you are ready to serve your guests.

CANDIED FRUIT

TANGHULU 冰糖葫芦

My grandmother, Lily, popped a skewer of candied cherry into her mouth and smiled with satisfaction.

'That sweetness just went right through me and gave me shivers. It was so sweet. But oh, so good!'

China was one of the first nations to discover sugar preservation methods and this technique of candying fruit has existed since the 14th century. The Arabs developed the method and it was known in Europe by the 16th century. To make these on a commercial scale, the fruits are normally bathed for days in the syrup. However, for the purposes of home cooking, we've simplified the method.

150g/5½oz/¾ cup sugar

200ml/7fl oz/generous ¾ cup water

12 seedless grapes (about 115g/4oz)

4 cherries, cut in half and pitted

Skewer the fruit on four wooden skewers, putting three grapes and a cherry on each skewer.

Combine the sugar and water in a heavy saucepan over a high heat until bubbling. Be very careful as this mixture is extremely hot and can easily burn you. The syrup will form big bubbles, but don't stir. Turn off the heat.

Carefully coat the fruit skewers in the syrup to glaze all the fruit. Leave to cool completely on a sheet of baking parchment.

Lisa's tip These candied fruits are perfect to decorate cakes or desserts. You can also use other fruit, such as whole strawberries or kiwi fruit, cut into small pieces.

SERVES 4

PREP TIME
5 MINUTES, PLUS
2 HOURS SETTING
COOK TIME
5 MINUTES

RED BEAN JELLY

HONG DOU GUO DONG 红豆果冻

We stumbled across a fruit and vegetable market in China, where things are on a much bigger scale than in the UK. Rows of red beans were laid out on tarpaulins the size of a marquee. On closer inspection the beans were reddish-brown with a cream strip on one side.

'What are they?' I asked Lisa.

'Adzuki beans. You'll know them as the red bean paste we get in cans.'

'Wow. I never knew that red bean paste came from such beans.'

'Neither did I,' said Lisa, 'until I read the sign over there!'

We use red bean paste a lot in our cooking – for mooncakes, cake fillings, sweet dessert soups, and in this instance for jellies.

100g/3½oz/½ cup sugar, dissolved in a little hot water

600ml/20fl oz/2½ cups cold water

100ml/3½fl oz/scant ½ cup whole milk

100ml/3½fl oz/scant ½ cup evaporated milk

300g/10½oz red bean paste

6 leaves of gelatine, soaked in cold water for 5 minutes

vegetable oil for the moulds

Mix all the ingredients, except the gelatine, in a food processor. Pour the mixture into a saucepan, add the softened gelatine and stir over a medium heat for 5 minutes until the mixture thickens slightly.

Cool the mixture by placing the pan in a bowl of ice cubes and cold water, stirring the mixture frequently.

Meanwhile, oil four small moulds, then pour the mixture into the moulds and put in the fridge for 2 hours until set.

Turn out of the moulds and serve chilled.

Lisa's tip You can use 16–20 tiny moulds to make these as petits fours.

RED BEAN COOKIES

HONG DOU BING GAN 紅豆餅乾

At one street market we saw a little boy, about five years old, being scolded by his mother: 'Behave yourself or you will not get your red bean cookie.' We watched them as they headed over to a stall where an elderly lady was serving. The boy pointed to the freshly baked cookies and his mum bought one for him. I went to get a portion of cookies for myself and as soon as I took a bite I could see why the little boy loved them so much. *Illustrated on previous spread.*

Bean filling

5 tbsp red bean paste

1 tbsp water

1 tsp vanilla extract

1 tsp coconut oil

pinch of salt

1 tsp sugar

Pastry

85g/3oz/scant ¾ cup plain (all-purpose) flour, plus extra for dusting

¼ tsp baking powder

3 tbsp golden syrup

3 tbsp coconut oil

2 tbsp vegetable oil, plus extra for greasing

1 tbsp sesame seeds (optional)

Preheat the oven to 180°C/350°F/gas 4. Grease a large baking sheet.

To make the filling, mix all the ingredients in a saucepan over a medium heat for 5 minutes until they combine to form a smooth paste. Set aside in a bowl to cool.

To make the pastry, mix the flour, baking powder, golden syrup and both oils together to form a dough; knead for 15 minutes. Dust a work surface with flour and roll out the dough thinly. Using a 6cm/2½in diameter pastry cutter, cut out eight discs. Place a teaspoon of the filling in the centre of each disc, then fold the dough over to form a semi-circle. Press down and flatten slightly. Sprinkle with sesame seeds, place on the baking sheet and bake for 15–20 minutes until golden brown. Transfer to a wire rack to cool.

Lisa's tip The filling could also be used to make red bean truffles: roll it into small balls and then roll the balls in cocoa powder.

MAKES 12

PREP TIME
30 MINUTES, PLUS
2 HOURS RISING AND
RESTING
COOK TIME
20–30 MINUTES

COILED PANCAKE

YOU XUAN 油旋

In Jinan, the capital of Shandong province, a food vendor was selling these unusual coiled breads. They were slightly oily and salty with a hint of sweetness, and reminded me of a thick croissant. *Illustrated on previous spread.*

2 tsp dried yeast

5 tsp caster (superfine) sugar

1 tsp salt

5 tbsp lukewarm water

250g/9oz/2 cups plain (all-purpose) flour, plus extra for dusting

200ml/7fl oz/generous ¾ cup soya milk, warmed

1 tbsp vegetable oil

150g/5½oz/⅔ cup unsalted butter, chilled, cut into small dice

1 egg yolk, beaten

In a small bowl, mix the yeast, sugar, salt and water until frothy. Sift the flour into a large bowl and add the warm milk and vegetable oil. Gradually add the yeast mixture and knead for about 10 minutes to make a smooth dough. Cover the bowl with clingfilm and leave in a warm place for about 1 hour until the dough has doubled in size.

Roll out the dough on a floured work surface to make a 30cm/12in square; it should be about 1cm/½ in thick. Dot the butter evenly over the dough and fold the left to the centre, fold the right to the centre, fold the top to the centre and fold the bottom to the centre to make a parcel. Turn the dough 90 degrees and repeat the rolling and folding twice more. Wrap in clingfilm and put in the fridge for 1 hour.

Preheat the oven to 180°C/350°F/gas 4.

Roll out the dough into a thin 30cm/12in square. Cut into 12 strips and roll each strip into a tight coil. Brush with egg yolk. Bake for 20–30 minutes until golden brown and the coils have expanded. Serve warm.

Lisa's tip If you like chocolate, you can spread the pancakes with Nutella.

SERVES 4 (MAKES 16)

PREP TIME
20 MINUTES, PLUS
20 MINUTES RESTING
COOK TIME
10 MINUTES

THREE BIG GUNSHOTS

SĀN DÀ PÀO 三大炮

If you go to Chengdu, the capital of Sichuan province, you'll most probably end up on Wenshufang Street. It was there that I learnt about this street snack, evocatively nicknamed 'three big cannons'. I was drawn to the street vendor by the noise he was making. Part of the process and fun of making these rice balls is throwing them against a metal tray, causing the bang. The burly chef chuckled as he mimicked the sound. 'Bang, bang, bang. Like cannon.' And he continued to throw the balls hard – to draw attention to his wares. Soon enough his antics worked and I bought a portion – anything to get a bit of peace and quiet!

They were coated in a sweet syrup and dusted with sesame flour. Delicious and sickly at the same time. The next vendor was selling *Laoying* tea (also known as 'eagle tea'), a herbal tea which was a perfect accompaniment and helped to cut the sweetness of this popular dessert.

150g/5½oz/scant 1 cup glutinous rice flour, sifted

2 tbsp rice flour

1 tbsp custard powder

200ml/7fl oz/generous ¾ cup skimmed milk

200ml/7fl oz/generous ¾ cup coconut milk

70g/2½oz/⅓ cup caster (superfine) sugar

1 tbsp vegetable oil, plus extra for greasing

5 tbsp golden syrup

2 tbsp sesame flour (or sesame seeds)

Sift both rice flours and the custard powder into a heatproof bowl.

In a saucepan, combine the milk, coconut milk, sugar and oil and bring to the boil over a high heat. Then turn down the heat and simmer for 5 minutes. Pour the milk mixture into the flour and mix to a stiff dough.

Half-fill a wok with hot water and put a trivet or round cake rack in the wok. Put the bowl of dough on the trivet, cover the wok with a lid and steam over a medium–high heat for 20 minutes to cook the dough.

Divide the cooked dough into 16 equal portions. Roll into balls in the palms of your hands. Dip in the golden syrup and then roll in the sesame flour or sesame seeds.

Serve with a cup of Chinese tea.

Lisa's tip You can keep these for up to a week in an airtight container before dipping in the syrup.

PORTUGUESE EGG TARTS

PU SHI DAN TA 葡式蛋撻

You might be puzzled as to why Portuguese egg tarts feature in this book. Well, Macao, on the southern coast of China, not far from Hong Kong, was once a colony of Portugal. When the Portuguese introduced their egg tarts, the traditional *pastel de nata*, to the Macao region the local Chinese loved them. We always enjoy a couple of these delicious snacks when we visit Macao.

4 free-range egg yolks

100g/3½oz/½ cup caster (superfine) sugar

40g/1½oz/¼ cup potato starch

2 vanilla pods, cut lengthways and seeds scraped out

200ml/7fl oz/generous ¾ cup whole milk

250ml/9fl oz/1 cup double (heavy) cream

butter, for greasing

flour, for dusting

300g/10½oz ready-rolled puff pastry

icing (confectioners') sugar, for dusting

Put the egg yolks, sugar and potato starch in a saucepan over a low heat and stir continuously for 5 minutes or until thickened. Add the vanilla seeds, milk and cream and whisk continuously until the mixture becomes a smooth custard. Bring to the boil, then turn off the heat and transfer to a bowl to cool. Cover with clingfilm to prevent a skin from forming.

Preheat the oven to 180°C/350°F/gas 4. Grease a 12-hole tart tin with butter.

Lightly dust a work surface with flour and roll out the pastry to about 3mm/⅛in thick. Using a 8cm/3in diameter pastry cutter, cut out 12 rounds and place in the tart tin. Fill with the cooled custard. Bake for 20 minutes or until the custard is golden brown. Dust with icing sugar and serve warm.

Lisa's tip These are also delicious cold and perfect to serve with Bubble Tea (page 180).

MAKES 10

PREP TIME
30 MINUTES, PLUS 1
HOUR CHILLING
COOK TIME
25 MINUTES

EGG TARTS

DAN TA 蛋撻

This is my niece Katherine's favourite dessert. Some of her first words were '*dan ta*'. She particularly loved the egg custard and would just eat the filling and leave the crust. We had to encourage her to eat the whole thing as no one really wanted her leftovers! You can make this with puff pastry, or with the firmer pastry crust given here.

Crust

150g/5½oz/1¼ cups plain (all-purpose) flour, plus extra for dusting

1 tsp baking powder

2 tsp custard powder

100ml/3½fl oz/scant ½ cup water

½ tsp salt

50g/1¾oz/4 tbsp unsalted butter, diced, plus extra for greasing

Egg custard

3 eggs

200ml/7fl oz/generous ¾ cup whole or semi-skimmed milk

100g/3½oz/½ cup caster (superfine) sugar

1 tbsp evaporated milk

1 tsp vanilla extract

Sift the flour into a large bowl and add the rest of the crust ingredients. Mix and knead to make a smooth, pliable dough. Cover with clingfilm and leave in the fridge while you make the filling.

To make the custard, beat the eggs in a bowl. Put the milk and sugar into a small saucepan and stir over a medium heat for 3–4 minutes until the sugar has dissolved. Pour the hot milk over the beaten eggs and whisk together. Add the evaporated milk and vanilla extract and whisk again until smooth. Cover the bowl with clingfilm and transfer to the fridge to chill for 1 hour.

Preheat the oven to 200°/400°F/gas 6. Grease ten aluminium egg tart moulds with butter.

Dust a work surface with flour and roll out the dough to about 3mm/⅛in thick. Cut out ten circles and place one in each of the moulds. Pour the chilled egg custard into the moulds until they are just over three-quarters full – allow some room for the custard to rise. Place on a baking sheet and bake for 15 minutes, then reduce the oven temperature to 180°C/350°F/gas 4 and bake for a further 5 minutes. Turn off the oven and leave the custard tarts in the oven for a further 5 minutes until they are fully set. To serve, remove the tarts from the moulds and serve warm.

Lisa's tip These are also great served cold with a cup of jasmine tea. Perfect to pack for the lunchbox.

OLD-SCHOOL CANTONESE GLUTINOUS RICE BALLS

NUO MI CI 糯米糍

These are one of my favourite desserts. When we were growing up they were a little treat when we had been good. When Dad was buying the stock for the shop, we waited patiently in the car and honked the horn when we saw a traffic warden. To reward us, Dad always bought us one of these and I have continued to buy them ever since.

150g/5½oz/scant 1 cup glutinous
   rice flour

1 tbsp custard powder

200ml/7fl oz/generous ¾ cup coconut milk

70g/2½oz/⅓ cup caster (superfine) sugar

1 tbsp vegetable oil, plus extra for greasing

Peanut filling

200g/7oz/1⅓ cups raw peanuts,
   lightly toasted, then finely chopped

350g/12oz/3¾ cups desiccated coconut

100g/3½oz/⅔ cup sesame seeds

85g/3oz/scant ½ cup caster (superfine)
   sugar

Sift the flour and custard powder into a bowl. Combine the coconut milk, sugar and oil in a saucepan and bring to the boil over a high heat. Reduce the heat and simmer for 5 minutes. Pour the hot milk over the flour and mix to a stiff dough. Place the dough in a greased heatproof bowl and put the bowl inside a bamboo steamer basket.

Put a trivet or round cake rack in a wok and add boiling water so that it is just over a quarter full. Put the steamer basket on the trivet, cover and steam for 20 minutes. Remove from the steamer and set aside to cool.

To make the peanut filling, combine the peanuts, 150g/5oz/1⅔ cups of the desiccated coconut, the sesame seeds and sugar in a bowl and set aside.

Turn the steamed dough out onto a work surface and divide into 16 equal portions. Roll into balls in the palms of your hands. Flatten each ball and roll out to a circle, approx. 8cm/3in in diameter, using a rolling pin. Place 1 heaped tablespoon of the peanut filling in the centre of each circle and draw up the dough around the sides to enclose the filling. Mould into a ball. Repeat to form 16 balls.

Put the remaining coconut on a plate. Dip the filled balls in water and then roll them in the coconut, coating them on all sides. Serve in cupcake cases.

Lisa's tip Instead of coating them in coconut, you could dip then in cocoa powder or hundreds and thousands (sugar sprinkles).

COCONUT MILK WITH TAPIOCA

YE RU MU SHU 椰乳木薯

When we returned to Hong Kong with my grandmother in 2002 we saw a vendor selling this dessert and she told us, 'During World War II food was so scarce in Hong Kong that I had to eat this mush for days on end. Look at it now – it's the trendy dessert and people love it!'

Tapioca is made from cassava and is not a grain, so it is naturally gluten free.

100g/3½oz/⅔ cup tapioca, soaked in hot
   water for 40 minutes

400ml/14fl oz/1⅔ cups coconut milk

2 tsp sugar

1 tsp vanilla extract

fresh fruit such as mango, to serve
   (optional)

Heat the coconut milk in a saucepan and add the tapioca, sugar and vanilla. Bring to the boil for 5 minutes then reduce the heat and simmer for a further 15 minutes. This will thicken the coconut milk and the tapioca will become translucent.

Serve hot, with fresh fruit if you wish.

Lisa's tip Any leftovers can be enjoyed cold; store in the fridge until required.

EGG WAFFLE PUFFS

JI DAN ZAI 鸡蛋仔

When we visited Hong Kong we squealed with delight at the 'edible bubble wrap'. These are now so popular that many supermarkets have a vendor at the entrance creating these egg puffs in various flavours, including vanilla, strawberry, chocolate, green tea and coconut. The first thing that hits you is its sweet egg aroma, which makes your stomach rumble. Pulling each 'egg' off the piece is particularly enjoyable and it's best to consume when hot off the press. It's very satisfying to bite into the warm puff, hearing the edges crunch and enjoying the chewy texture in the middle. The vendor told us that these originated from an egg seller in the 1950s. Rather than discard the broken eggs he made these waffle-like egg puffs and eventually created a mould that made egg shapes rather than the usual waffle shape. If you have a silicone mini-cake (cake pop) mould then that would create a similar shape if you make these in the oven. Failing that, use your waffle maker and a sprinkling of imagination.

2 eggs

50g/1¾oz/¼ cup caster (superfine) sugar

150ml/5floz/⅔ cup whole or semi-skimmed milk

3 tbsp water

150g/5½oz/1¼ cups plain (all-purpose) flour

2 tsp custard powder

1 tsp baking powder

2 tsp vanilla extract

2 tbsp vegetable oil, plus extra for greasing

In a bowl, mix the eggs, sugar, milk and water. Add the flour, custard powder, baking powder and vanilla, then add the oil and mix to a smooth batter.

Grease your waffle maker or egg puff mould with oil and heat the mould. Pour in the batter, close the mould, and place it over a medium heat until the batter cooks through, turning once – about 1 minute on each side. Use a knife or a fork to dislodge the egg puffs and serve warm.

Lisa's tip If you like, you can dust these with icing (confectioners') sugar or serve with ice cream. Indeed this mixture could be used to make ice cream cones.

ROASTED CHESTNUTS

KAO LI ZI 烤栗子

I remember being in Shanghai during December; I was freezing and aching to get home. But the bus was taking ages to arrive and I began to lose the feeling in my toes. Then I saw a woman selling chestnuts. The smoke was billowing and a crowd of hungry and cold travellers had gathered – probably also waiting for the bus. I made a beeline for her and slowly edged my way in towards the warmth. She thrust a bag of chestnuts into my hand and wanted a yuan. I paid her gladly and enjoyed the chestnuts and the warmth of her fire. They were so simple, yet so delicious and satisfying.

The downside to cooking chestnuts is that if they are not properly cooked through they are hard and not very nice to eat. If you are unsure, cut one open and if you can squeeze the flesh out then it's ready to eat. Chestnuts are extremely robust and it takes a long time for them to burn – and it doesn't matter if the shell burns, because you peel it off before eating the nut.

1kg/2lb 4oz chestnuts

Preheat the oven to 200°/400°F/gas 6. Score each chestnut with a cross to help them cook through and place them on a baking sheet. Cook for 30 minutes or until the chestnuts are soft. Enjoy warm.

Lisa's tip Sprinkle some ground cinnamon over the chestnuts when you put them into the oven to give an added dimension.

SERVES 2

PREP TIME
15 MINUTES, PLUS UP
TO 2 HOURS SETTING
COOK TIME
0 MINUTES

MANGO PUDDING

MANG GUO BU DING 芒果布丁

Mango pudding is a popular dessert in China. It's not really a 'pudding' – the texture is more like a crème brûlée or egg custard – light, airy and sweet – but it's everything your sweet tooth desires.

1 large fresh mango

100ml/3½fl oz/scant ½ cup
 evaporated milk

5 tbsp caster (superfine) sugar

6 leaves of gelatine, soaked in cold water
 for 5 minutes

150g/5½oz canned mango slices, blended
 in a food processor

10 ice cubes

2 sprigs of mint, to decorate

Cut the mango in half. Dice the flesh of one half. Set aside the other half to use for decoration.

Heat the evaporated milk and sugar in a small saucepan over a low heat until the sugar has dissolved. Add the softened gelatine leaves and stir gently to dissolve.

In a bowl, mix together the blended mango and diced fresh mango. Add the evaporated milk and gelatine mixture. Add the ice cubes and stir until the ice has melted and the mixture has thickened slightly. Pour into two jelly moulds, 10cm/4in in diameter. Transfer to the fridge to set for 1½–2 hours.

To serve, turn out the puddings onto a serving plate and decorate with a few slices of fresh mango and sprigs of mint.

Lisa's tip If you want a mix of flavours you can add diced banana or lychees to the gelatine mixture as well as the diced fresh mango.

BOWL PUDDING

WAN BU DING 碗布丁

We had to search high and low for a bowl pudding in China. We were determined to find this recipe because our father is nicknamed after this dessert. This dessert is heavy, stodgy, extremely sweet and dense – arguably a bit like Dad, according to Mum! Tastes in China are moving away from this old-fashioned style of pudding to healthier options, but it is still a firm favourite among the older generation.

In Shenzen we found an old man with a face full of deep wrinkles, further accentuated by his deep tan, who was steaming these in disposable foil cups.

'One, please.'

'$5,' he said, with a toothless but boyish grin. We paid him and he tipped one of the puddings into a bowl and stuck two toothpicks into it as makeshift chopsticks. A jelly-like dessert would usually break when lifted with a toothpick but this was so dense that it sat securely on the toothpicks. It was delicious. Lisa motioned for me to share.

'Get your own, Lisa!' I exclaimed. We chuckled and ordered one more.

4 tbsp dried red beans (adzuki beans), soaked for 2–3 hours
vegetable oil for the moulds
2 tbsp dark brown sugar
50g/1¾oz/5 tbsp rice flour
200ml/7fl oz/generous ¾ cup hot water
coconut milk and fruit, to serve

Drain the beans and put them in a saucepan with plenty of water to cover them. Bring to the boil, then simmer for 1 hour or until softened. Drain and set aside.

Oil four small moulds or pudding bowls.

Put the sugar, rice flour and hot water in a saucepan and mix thoroughly. Divide among the four moulds. Add a tablespoon of the cooked beans to each mould.

Put the moulds in a bamboo steamer basket and steam for 20 minutes until cooked; to test, stick a toothpick or cocktail stick in the middle and if it comes out clean then it is cooked. Leave to cool.

Turn out of the moulds and serve with coconut milk and fruit.

SERVES 4

PREP TIME
10 MINUTES, PLUS
2 HOURS CHILLING
COOK TIME
0 MINUTES

GRASS JELLY

LIANG FEN 涼粉

'What's that black stuff in the glass?' I asked the vendor.

'Grass jelly.'

'What, jelly made out of grass?'

'Sort of. But the 'grass' is *Mesona chinensis*, a member of the mint family,' replied the vendor. She offered some to me and I tentatively took a bit and nibbled at it cautiously. 'Hmm, it's a bit bitter but it has a hint of lavender. It's OK. I guess it's an acquired taste.'

50g/1¾oz grass jelly powder

60g/2¼oz/5 tbsp sugar

2 leaves of gelatine, soaked in cold water for 5 minutes

200ml/7fl oz/generous ¾ cup hot water

600ml/20fl oz/2½ cups cold water

sugar syrup, coconut milk or fruit, to serve (optional)

Dissolve the grass jelly powder, sugar and softened gelatine leaves in the hot water. Add the cold water and mix thoroughly. Pour into a mould and leave to set in the fridge for 2 hours.

To serve, cut the jelly into cubes and, if you like, serve with sugar syrup (dissolve 4 tablespoons sugar in 4 tablespoons water), coconut milk or fruit.

Lisa's tip Grass jelly can be bought in a can but I find it more satisfying to make my own. It means I can adjust the amount of sugar, and if making it for vegetarian guests, a vegetarian gelling agent can be used instead of gelatine.

SERVES 4

PREP TIME
15 MINUTES, PLUS
COOLING AND
FREEZING
COOK TIME
0 MINUTES

SNOW ICE

XUE HUA BING 雪花冰

There was a loud vibrating sound coming from the next stall. I turned to see people holding bowls of colourful snow ice, shaved from the round frozen block by this noisy machine. I was amazed how many flavours this stall offered, some of them garnished with sweetcorn kernels or sweet red beans – popular in China. My favourite flavour was lychee, which I've re-created here.

300ml/10fl oz/1¼ cups milk

400ml/14fl oz/1⅔ cups coconut milk

300ml10fl oz/1¼ cups lychee juice

100g/3½oz fresh lychees, peeled and blitzed in a food processor

4 tbsp caster (superfine) sugar

1 tsp vanilla extract

4 tbsp Lychee Jelly (page 164) (optional)

4 tbsp Grass Jelly (page 153) (optional)

3 fresh strawberries, chopped, to serve

Heat the milk, coconut milk, lychee juice, puréed lychees, sugar and vanilla extract in a saucepan and bring to the boil. Pour into a freezerproof container and leave to cool, then place in the freezer for 3–4 hours.

To create the snow ice effect, use a fork to scrape the frozen dessert into bowls. Serve with a spoonful of lychee jelly and a spoonful of grass jelly, if you like, or some fresh strawberries.

Lisa's tips Lychee juice drink is widely available, although some contain more actual lychee juice than others: look for one with at least 15–20% lychee juice.

Instead of lychees, you can make this with mangoes, passionfruit, peaches or strawberries.

STEAMED SWEET EGG

JIDAN GENG 蒸甜蛋

This is one of our sweetest childhood memories. On a cold winter's morning, Mum used to get up before dawn to make this for us. We were not good at waking up and tried to sleep for as long as we could – so much so that one night we wore our school uniforms (ties included) to bed so we could just get up and go. When Mum found out – quite obvious as we looked so dishevelled – she shook her head and told us we couldn't take shortcuts in life: anything worthwhile would take time and patience. She used this dish as an example. The custard was smooth and sweet, perfect every time. One day, while we were eating, she demonstrated how it would be if made in haste – and it was bobbly, rough and unappetizing. Mum ended up eating that version and it really hit home. After that day, we tried our best to get up in time to dress properly rather than rushing. I confess I still find it hard to wake up early, but when I eat this dish I remember us standing there in our crumpled uniforms with mum shaking her head. This dish is dedicated to our mum.

4 large eggs, beaten with a fork
300ml/10fl oz/1¼ cups cold water
3 tbsp caster (superfine) sugar

Strain the beaten eggs through a sieve into a bowl. Add the water and sugar and whisk for about 5 minutes until the mixture is frothy and aerated. Pour the mixture into two ramekins or bowls and put the ramekins inside a bamboo steamer basket.

Put a large trivet or round cake rack in a wok and add boiling water so that it is just over a quarter full. Put the steamer basket on the trivet, cover and steam over a low heat for 15 minutes until the mixture is firm. To check that it's fully cooked insert a wooden cocktail stick into the centre of the mixture. If it comes out clean and no liquid rises to the top of the ramekin then it is ready to serve.

Lisa's tip You can make a savoury version of this dish using chicken, pork, prawns and spring onions. The raw meats should be cut into small pieces and added to the whisked egg mixture: they will take the same time to cook. Replace the water with chicken stock for added flavour..

SERVES 4

PREP TIME
20 MINUTES, PLUS
10 MINUTES SOAKING
COOK TIME
20 MINUTES

RICE BALLS WITH GINGER SYRUP

FAN TUAN 飯糰

These rice balls are very simple to make, but on their own they are flavourless, so we enjoy them in a ginger-flavoured syrup. We eat them at Chinese New Year and their shape symbolizes the unity of the family on this very important day. I remember making these with my mum when I was growing up – laughing about the big feast we would be enjoying the next day – such sweet memories.

200g/7oz/1¼ cups glutinous rice flour
150ml/5floz/⅔ cup water

Ginger syrup
250ml/9fl oz/1 cup water
70g/2½oz/⅓ cup caster (superfine) sugar
4cm/1½in piece of fresh root ginger

Mix the rice flour with the water to form a soft dough. Knead for about 10 minutes until it is smooth, then shape the dough into small balls, making approximately 32.

Half-fill a saucepan with boiling water, add the rice balls and simmer for 5 minutes. They will float to the surface when they are cooked. Drain in a colander.

To make the ginger syrup, put the water, sugar and ginger in a saucepan over a medium heat for about 10–15 minutes until the sugar has dissolved and the ginger flavour has infused into the syrup. Remove from the heat and add the drained rice balls to soak in the flavour for 10 minutes. Serve the rice balls in a bowl with the ginger syrup.

Lisa's tip Instead of the ginger syrup, serve the rice balls with coconut milk instead.

PANDAN SWISS ROLL

XIANG LAN RUI SHI JUAN 香兰瑞士卷

This is a wonderful family get-together recipe, and one that children enjoy cooking. It's lighter than the usual chocolate or raspberry jam swiss roll and the pandan flavour is subtle, slightly aniseed. The best way to extract the flavour and green colour of pandan is from the leaves, which you chop, blend with a little water and strain through a sieve. However, they are hard to come by so we have used pandan extract in this recipe. In China, pandan rolls are usually taken as a gift when visiting friends and family during Chinese New Year. Many small bakeries have popped up at stations, so when people arrive at their destination they can buy a chilled pandan roll, ready to serve.

2 tbsp unsalted butter, for greasing

4 eggs, separated

85g/3oz/scant ½ cup caster (superfine) sugar

1 tsp cream of tartar

1 tsp vanilla extract

2 tsp pandan extract

85g/3oz/scant ¾ cup self-raising flour, sifted

125ml/4floz/½ cup double (heavy) cream

4 tbsp icing (confectioners') sugar, plus extra for dusting

Preheat the oven to 180°/350°F/gas 4. Grease and line a 23 x 30cm/9 x 12in shallow baking tin, then grease the baking parchment with the butter.

In a freestanding mixer, whisk the egg whites with the caster sugar, cream of tartar and vanilla extract for 10 minutes until stiff peaks form. Then add the egg yolks and pandan extract and whisk for 1 minute. Fold in the sifted flour a little at a time until it's fully mixed in.

Pour the mixture into the prepared tin and spread it evenly over the parchment. Bake for 10 minutes until just firm to the touch. Test by inserting a wooden cocktail stick into the sponge: if it comes out clean the cake is cooked. Put the baking tin on a wire rack and leave to cool slightly. Turn out onto a piece of baking parchment, then peel off the baking parchment.

Whip the cream with the icing sugar until firm. Spread evenly over the sponge. Using the parchment to hold the sponge and cream in place, roll forward to create a swiss roll effect. Chill until ready to eat. Dust with icing sugar before serving.

Lisa's tip Feel free to add some fruit, such as blueberries, and/or chopped nuts into the whipped cream.

SERVES 8–10

PREP TIME
15 MINUTES, PLUS
24 HOURS SETTING
COOK TIME
10–15 MINUTES

NOUGAT

NIU ZHA TANG 牛軋糖

This is a white nougat similar to Italian torrone. It's laden with nuts, chewy rather than hard, with a crisp rice-paper base. You will need a free-standing food mixer and a sugar thermometer.

500g/1lb 2oz almonds, crushed

50g/1¾oz hazelnuts, chopped

5 tbsp clear honey

200g/7oz/1 cup caster (superfine) sugar

3 egg whites

1 tsp vanilla extract

rice paper, to line the tin

Line a small square cake tin (approx. 15 x 15cm/6 x 6in) with rice paper.

Put the almonds and hazelnuts in a dry saucepan over a medium heat for 2 minutes, until lightly toasted. Set aside.

Heat the honey in a bain-marie, stirring continuously. Heat the sugar gently in a small saucepan, then add to the honey and continue to heat until the temperature reaches 125°C/260°F on a sugar thermometer.

In a mixer, whisk the egg whites until they form stiff peaks. Gradually and carefully add the honey and sugar mixture and the vanilla extract, whisking continuously; the mixture will thicken. Stir in the nuts and pour into the cake tin. Cover with a sheet of baking parchment and level the mixture. Leave to set for 24 hours.

Cut the nougat into squares to serve.

Lisa's tip Whenever you are cooking sugar to a high heat please be extra careful as it can burn and cause serious injury.

SERVES 4

PREP TIME
20 MINUTES, PLUS
1 HOUR CHILLING
COOK TIME
15 MINUTES,
PLUS COOLING

TOFU FA PUDDING

DOU FU HUA 豆腐花

Tofu, which is made from soya beans, is to the Chinese is what cheese is to the French, a national treasure. Prince Liu An, the grandson of Emperor Liu Bang, is credited with its discovery, during the Han dynasty. Legend has it that he was searching for an elixir of immortality, but instead he discovered how to coagulate soya bean milk into tender white curds. In this recipe the soya milk is set with gelatine and accompanied with ginger syrup, which imparts elements of heat and sweetness.

5 tbsp water

7g/¼oz packet of powdered gelatine

1 litre/1¾ pints/4 cups soya milk

40g/1½oz/3 tbsp caster (superfine) sugar

Ginger syrup
150g/5½oz/¾ cup soft light brown sugar

2cm/¾in piece of fresh root ginger, cut into strips

150ml/5floz/⅔ cup water

½ tsp salt

Put the water in a small bowl, sprinkle the gelatine over the surface, and whisk with a fork. Stand the bowl in a larger bowl of hot water and set aside for 10 minutes, stirring occasionally until the gelatine has dissolved.

Put the soya milk and sugar in a saucepan and stir over a high heat for 10 minutes until the sugar has dissolved. Reduce the heat to low and whisk in the dissolved gelatine. Strain the mixture through a sieve into a shallow container, cool and leave in the fridge for 1 hour until set.

To make the ginger syrup, put the sugar, ginger and water in a saucepan over a high heat and boil rapidly for 5 minutes until the sugar has dissolved and the syrup darkened slightly. Add the salt, and then remove the pan from the heat. Set aside to cool and thicken.

To serve, use a large spoon to place 2–3 slices of the *tofu fa* onto each plate. Add 5 tablespoons of the ginger syrup over each portion.

Lisa's tip For a low-sugar option you can omit the ginger syrup and serve the *tofu fa* plain or with fresh fruit.

HANGZHOU'S CANDIED LOTUS ROOT

HANG ZHOU MI OU 杭州蜜藕

Walking around Hangzhou and admiring the sights I was feeling slightly peckish. I came across a stall selling candied lotus root and was intrigued as I had never tried these before. They were sweet yet savoury, as lotus root has a distinctive, slightly earthy taste.

1 litre/1¾ pints/4 cups water

85g/3oz/scant ½ cup caster (superfine) sugar, plus extra for coating

2 tbsp white vinegar

½ tsp salt

2cm/¾in piece of fresh root ginger, peeled and sliced

100g/3½oz cooked lotus roots, finely sliced

Put the water, sugar, vinegar, salt and ginger in a saucepan and boil for 5 minutes. Add the lotus roots and turn the heat down to low for 20 minutes. The lotus roots will absorb most of the sugar syrup.

Carefully lift the lotus root slices onto a piece of baking parchment and sprinkle both sides with sugar to coat evenly. Leave until cold.

Lisa's tip These are perfect for snacks. Store in an airtight container.

SERVES 4

PREP TIME
20 MINUTES, PLUS
2 HOURS CHILLING
COOK TIME
10 MINUTES

LYCHEE JELLY

LI ZHI ZHE LI 荔枝啫喱

Lychees grow in southern China, especially in Guangzhou province, where the beautiful red fruit is seen in abundance in the summer months. Inside their bumpy skin the aromatic white fruit is bursting with sweet, refreshing juice.

10g konnyaku (konjac) powder
(or 2 tbsp powdered gelatine)

3 tbsp fresh lychee juice

60g/2¼oz/5 tbsp caster (superfine) sugar

250ml/9fl oz/1 cup boiling water

425g can of lychees, drained and chopped
into small pieces

If using gelatine, put 3 tablespoons water in a small bowl, sprinkle the gelatine over the surface, and whisk with a fork. Stand the bowl in a larger bowl of hot water and set aside for 10 minutes, stirring occasionally, until the gelatine has dissolved.

Put the lychee juice, sugar and water in a saucepan and stir over a medium heat until the sugar has dissolved. Add the konnyaku powder (or the dissolved gelatine) and stir continuously until the mixture comes to the boil. Pour into a shallow container, about 18 x 18cm/7 x 7in (or whatever mould you wish to use) and scatter over the chopped lychees. Set aside to cool, then transfer the jelly to the fridge to chill for 2 hours.

Slice the jelly into 2.5cm/1in cubes. Serve with Chinese Iced Lemon Tea (see page 182).

Lisa's tip You could add this jelly to a cocktail or serve with Snow Ice (page 154).

SERVES 4

PREP TIME
20 MINUTES, PLUS
40 MINUTES RESTING
COOK TIME
40 MINUTES

STEAMED SPONGE CAKE

FA GAO 發糕

This is probably best eaten hot, straight from the steamer. It's light and perfect with a cup of Mango Milk (page 185) or coffee.

250g/9oz/2 cups plain (all-purpose) flour

50g/1¾oz/heaped ⅓ cup custard powder

2 tsp baking powder

2 tsp bicarbonate of soda (baking soda)

6 medium eggs

300g/10½oz/1½ cups brown sugar

2 tsp lard, melted, plus extra for greasing

1 tsp vanilla extract

1 tsp Cointreau

2 tsp grated orange zest

Sift the flour, custard powder, baking powder and bicarbonate of soda into a large bowl. Mix to combine evenly.

Crack the eggs into a separate bowl and whisk, using an electric whisk, until pale and frothy. Gradually add the sugar and beat until smooth and light. Add the egg mixture to the dry ingredients and mix well. Cover and set aside to rest for 30 minutes.

Add the melted lard and vanilla extract, Cointreau and orange zest and mix well. Leave to rest for a further 10 minutes.

Grease a 20cm/8in diameter round cake tin and line with baking parchment.

Pour the batter into the prepared cake tin and place the tin inside a large bamboo steamer. Place a trivet or round cake rack in a wok and fill the wok with boiling water so it is just over a quarter full. Cover the steamer basket with its lid, place on the trivet and steam over a high heat for 40 minutes. Turn off the heat and leave the cake in the steamer for 1 minute with the lid slightly ajar.

Cut the hot cake into generous slices and serve.

Lisa's tip This is great with a slather of marmalade and whipped cream.

MAKES 24

PREP TIME
30 MINUTES,
PLUS RESTING
COOK TIME
1 HOUR

PINEAPPLE TARTS

BO LUO TA 菠萝挞

I remember trekking around Hong Kong visiting our six aunties at Chinese New Year. As small children we had no idea who was who and the adults would sit for hours talking and playing mah-jong. However, the saving grace was these pineapple tarts. We'd nibble at the pastry and save the best bit – the filling – till last. Even today, when I stumble across a shop selling these, I find myself eating it in the same fashion. I guess old habits die hard!

Pastry

400g/14oz/3¼ cups plain (all-purpose) flour, plus extra for dusting

1 tbsp baking powder

½ tsp pinch of salt

200g/7oz/generous ¾ cup unsalted butter, chilled and cut into small dice, plus extra for greasing

4 tbsp caster (superfine) sugar

4 eggs, beaten, plus 1 extra to glaze (optional)

2 tsp vanilla extract

Filling

½ fresh pineapple, cut into small dice

100g/3½oz/½ cup brown sugar

½ tsp ground cinnamon

1 whole star anise

To make the pastry, sift the flour, baking powder and salt into a food processor, add the butter and pulse until it resembles fine breadcrumbs. Add the caster sugar, eggs and vanilla extract and mix for 3 minutes until it forms a dough; if it looks dry, add up to 5 tablespoons of cold water to bind the mixture together. Put the dough in a bowl, cover and chill for 30 minutes or so.

To make the filling, put the pineapple and brown sugar in a saucepan and cook over a high heat for about 45 minutes until it starts to turn brown and jam-like. Add the cinnamon and star anise and cook for a further 1 minute. Then take out the star anise.

Preheat the oven to 180°/350°F/gas 4. Grease a 12-hole tart tin with butter.

Lightly dust a work surface with flour and roll out the dough to about 5mm/¼in thick. Using a 8cm/3in diameter pastry cutter, cut out 12 rounds and place in the tart tin. Fill with the pineapple filling. If you like, you can decorate the top with four strips of dough in a lattice pattern. Glaze the dough strips with beaten egg. Bake for 15 minutes until the pastry is golden brown and the filling is oozing. Serve warm or cold.

Lisa's tip These are perfect for picnics or for parties. If you want a variety of fillings, try apricot or apple.

HONEYED LOTUS ROOT WITH STICKY RICE

MI OU NUO MI 蜜藕糯米

MAKES 4

PREP TIME
20 MINUTES, PLUS
2 HOURS SOAKING
COOK TIME
1 HOUR 20 MINUTES,
PLUS 15–20 MINUTES
TO GLAZE

The lotus root (botanically a rhizome) grows underwater and is usually eaten as a vegetable. It's starchy, sweet and crisp and when sliced its interior has a lacy pattern. You can occasionally find it in specialist vegetable merchants and Asian shops and markets. It is abundant in China, and it's the perfect street food because the gaps in the middle of the lotus roots can be filled with ingredients such as rice. When we visited Shanghai there were plenty of vendors selling these rice-filled lotus roots in a honey glaze – a wonderfully filling snack.

2 fresh lotus roots

85g/3oz/½ cup glutinous rice, washed and soaked in water for 2 hours

6 dried red dates (jujubes)

4 tbsp clear honey

Using a potato peeler, peel the lotus roots. Then cut a slice off one end of each root, exposing the holes within the root; reserve the end slice. Fill the holes with the glutinous rice, using a chopstick to push the rice down into each cavity. Put the reserved end slice back in place, using wooden skewers or cocktail sticks to secure it to the root, so the rice won't fall out during cooking.

Put the lotus roots in a saucepan and add enough cold water to cover the roots. Add the dried red dates, bring to the boil and boil for 1 hour.

Pour out two-thirds of the water, discard the dates and add the honey. Place over a medium–low heat, turning occasionally, for about 2 minutes until the honey coats the root in a glossy glaze. Slice the lotus roots into 1cm/½in pieces and serve.

Lisa's tip This goes really well with Citron Honey Tea (page 178).

DRINKS

饮料

TEA – GREEN, BLACK AND WHITE

CHA 茶

Tea is integral to Chinese history and food culture. It was served at tea houses along the Silk Road as a beverage for weary travellers and it was at these tea houses that dim sum (small bites made 'to touch the heart') were introduced. Today, throughout China, tea is served with meals; milk is never added.

There are many types of tea, made from the leaves of the tea plant, *Camellia sinensis*; and the word 'tea' is also used for infusions of other leaves and flowers. Tea is described by the way in which the tea leaves are processed (black, oolong, green, white), with many regional variations.

Many health benefits are attributed to tea because the leaves contain a number of polyphenols – compounds that are associated with, among other things, reduced risk of heart disease and stroke. As it is calorie-free and very refreshing, it is certainly the slimmer's friend.

Green tea has a long history; it is the earliest known method of processing the tea leaves.

Jasmine tea, a mix of jasmine flowers and green tea leaves, is probably the most popular type of tea in China. It's very fragrant and light in taste.

Black tea and oolong tea are strong in aroma and flavour. The tea leaves are allowed to oxidize (up to 70 per cent for oolong teas, and 100 per cent for black teas), often resulting in a smoky or cinnamon flavour with a bitter citrus aftertaste, like liquorice.

White tea refers to the way the tea leaves are processed, and makes a delicate pale yellow drink.

Chrysanthemum tea is made from chrysanthemum flowers; pale golden in colour, it is caffeine free and has a floral aroma. It can be drunk hot, and is also enjoyed cold, served with a few slices of orange and lemon.

Tea etiquette

Chinese people observe tea drinking etiquette on a daily basis. Tea is poured for all guests at the table before oneself; those receiving the tea will thank you by tapping one finger (if they are single) or two fingers (if they are married) on the table. This gesture is said to have originated in the time when China was ruled by imperial dynasties, and whenever the Emperor walked among his subjects, everyone had to kneel and bow. One day the Emperor wanted to go outside the Forbidden City to look at how his subjects were doing without their being aware of his identity, so he disguised himself in normal clothes. His bodyguards accompanied him and it was agreed that they'd use these finger gestures to 'bow' to the Emperor so as not to reveal his disguise.

Another point of tea etiquette, if you are in a restaurant and want more tea, is to remove the teapot lid and turn it upside down. The waiting staff will refill the teapot in response to this silent request.

24 HERBS TEA

CAO YAO CHA 草藥茶

SERVES 2

PREP TIME
15 MINUTES

24 herbs or 24 *mei* is the name given to a Cantonese herbal tea, drunk for medicinal purposes. Its name refers to the fact that it is a mixture of many different ingredients (around 24, although it may feature as few as 10 or as many as 28 or more). The recipe varies according to what ingredients you can get your hands on; the following list is a suggestion; ask a Chinese herbalist or look online. You can also buy a ready-blended 24 herbs tea to which you just add water. The tea is somewhat bitter in taste.

Typical ingredients

Mulberry leaf (桑叶)

Chrysanthemum flower (菊花)

Japanese honeysuckle flower (金银花)

Bamboo leaf (竹叶)

Peppermint (薄荷)

Imperata cylindrica (茅根)

Luohan guo (罗汉果)

Agastache rugosa (藿香)

Perilla frutescens (紫苏)

Elsholtzia (香薷)

Fermented soybean (淡豆鼓)

Cleistocalyx operculatus flower (水翁花)

Microcos paniculata leaf (布渣叶)

Ilex rotunda (救必应)

Put ¼ teaspoon of each of the herbs into a saucepan with 500ml/18fl oz/2 cups water and boil for 15 minutes. Strain and serve hot.

CITRON HONEY TEA

YOU ZI MI CHA 柚子蜜茶

SERVES 6–8

PREP TIME
5 MINUTES
COOK TIME
1 HOUR

This tea is full of vitamin C and is perfect if you are feeling under the weather. Note that no tea bags or tea leaves are used in this recipe, so it is a caffeine-free drink. Of course you can add actual tea if you want, but if you order this in China, this is what you'll get. *Illustrated on page 186.*

1 orange, sliced 5mm/¼in thick

1 lemon, sliced 5mm/¼in thick

3 tbsp honey

500ml/18fl oz/2 cups boiling water

Put the orange and lemon slices, honey and boiling water in a saucepan. Bring back to the boil, then reduce the heat to very low and simmer for about 1 hour.

Pour the syrup, with the orange and lemon slices, into a glass jar. (The syrup can be stored for up to 2 months.)

To make a glass of citron honey tea, put 1 tablespoon of the syrup into a glass, add approx. 150ml/5fl oz/⅔ cup of hot water and stir to mix.

Lisa's tip This drink can also be made with a slice of ginger to ease symptoms of colds or flu.

BUBBLE TEA

ZHEN ZHU NAI CHA 珍珠奶茶

SERVES 4

PREP TIME
5 MINUTES, PLUS
20–30 MINUTES
SOAKING

I find it impossible to walk past a bubble tea shop without stopping to buy one. The variety of colours and the aroma of the tea make it an irresistible treat: more than just a drink, it's almost a dessert. Bubble tea originated in Taiwan and is hugely popular in Hong Kong and China. The recipe below uses milky black tea, milkier and sweeter than English tea; it is often made with condensed milk. It is called bubble tea because the tea contains black tapioca 'bubbles', like large round beads, which are quite chewy – that is part of what makes bubble tea unique. Many bubble tea shops now offer a wide variety of flavoured tea bases and different flavours of bubbles such as lychee bubble and mango bubble. The flavourings are mainly from flavoured powders, but you can substitute syrups, such as those made by Monin.

50g/1¾oz dried bubble tea pearls

2 tbsp caster (superfine) sugar, plus extra to taste

3 strong tea bags

3 tbsp condensed milk

10–12 ice cubes

flavourings such as peach, lemon, pear, raspberry (optional)

Half-fill a saucepan with water, bring to the boil and add the dried bubbles. Turn off the heat and leave for 20–30 minutes; they will soften and become balls of black jelly.

Drain and while warm add the sugar; swirl the pan until the sugar has dissolved to give the bubbles flavour and a glossy sheen.

Use the tea bags to make a large pot of tea. Add the condensed milk to the tea, and add sugar to taste.

Pour the tea into glasses and cool it down by adding the ice cubes. Add some of the bubbles to each glass. If you like, add a flavouring and mix well. Add a large wide drinking straw and enjoy.

SOYA MILK DRINK

DÒUJIĀNG 豆浆

SERVES 4

PREP TIME
10 MINUTES
COOK TIME
45 MINUTES

In Beijing we tried a drink called *dòu zhi*; it is not for the faint-hearted – it's grey and tastes a bit off, like sour milk, with a grainy texture and a peculiar smell – but it's so popular among China's street food vendors that we had to try it. it is definitely a taste that has to be acquired before you can down the lot. Made from the water used to soak soya beans, it's apparently good for your digestive tract. Here is another soya bean-based drink – a bit more palatable.

150g/5½oz/¾ cup dried soya beans, soaked in water overnight

4 litres/7 pints/4 quarts water

2 tsp caster (superfine) sugar

Drain the soya beans, put them in a saucepan with the water and boil for 45 minutes.

Using a hand-held blender, or in a blender or food processor, blend the soya beans with the water for 5 minutes. Strain through a sieve: the resulting liquid is the soya milk. Add the sugar and stir well. Best served chilled.

ICED LEMON TEA

BING NING MENG CHA 冰檸檬茶

SERVES 2

PREP TIME
15 MINUTES

This is a classic Chinese drink which is very popular during the summer months as it is so refreshing. It uses fresh lemons, which give the drink its sharp flavour.

2 large lemons

550ml/about 1 pint/2¼ cups boiling water

1 strong tea bag

2 tsp caster (superfine) sugar

10 ice cubes

Cut two thin slices off one of the lemons and set aside to garnish. Using a vegetable peeler, peel the zest off the lemons in thin strips, leaving the white pith on the fruit. Squeeze the lemon juice.

Put 300ml/10fl oz/1¼ cups of the boiling water in a small saucepan with the lemon zest and juice and boil for 10 minutes. Strain and set aside.

Put the tea bag in a small tea pot, add 250ml/9fl oz/1 cup boiling water and leave to infuse for 2 minutes.

Put 1 teaspoon of sugar into each glass (or more if you like). Pour in the tea, dividing it equally between the glasses, and stir to dissolve the sugar. Add five ice cubes to each glass, pour in the lemon water and and a slice of lemon. Serve at once.

Lisa's tip Instead of boiling up the lemons you could stir a tablespoon of Monin lemon syrup into the iced tea.

LYCHEE VODKA

LI ZHI FU TE JIA 荔枝伏特加

MAKES 1

PREP TIME
5 MINUTES

Lychee vodka is a beautiful combination of the fragrant flavour of lychee and clean vodka. They pair well and make for an extra smooth cocktail. There are various brands of lychee juice drink: look for one with at least 15–20% lychee juice, such as Rubicon. Lychee wine is available from Asian or Chinese retailers.

50ml/2fl oz/3 tbsp vodka

25ml/1fl oz/1½ tbsp lychee wine

50ml/2fl oz/3 tbsp lychee juice

1 tbsp lime cordial

5 ice cubes

1 fresh or canned lychee,
    deseeded, to serve

Put all the ingredients into a cocktail shaker and shake for 3 minutes. Strain into a cocktail glass, garnish with a lychee on a cocktail stick and serve immediately.

WATERMELON JUICE

XI GUA ZHI 西瓜汁

SERVES 4

PREP TIME
5 MINUTES

Walking past a street stall in the blistering heat of Beijing, I saw a crowd of people and heard the whirring of a blender. The stall was selling fresh watermelon juice, a much-needed cooler in the city's heat. *Illustrated overleaf.*

½ a watermelon
100ml/3½fl oz/scant ½ cup water
ice cubes

Cut the rind off the watermelon and discard. Chop the flesh into pieces and put it into a juicer or blend briefly in a blender with the water. Strain to remove the pips. Put some ice cubes into four glasses, pour in the watermelon juice and serve at once.

PEAR AND JUJUBE JUICE

RE LI ZHI/ZAO ZHI 熱梨/棗汁

SERVES 2

PREP TIME
10 MINUTES

This is a very popular, warming drink which also is perfect as a light dessert. The jujube – also known as red date, Chinese date or Indian date – is a small date-like fruit that can be eaten fresh or dried. Japanese pears are also known as Chinese, Korean or nashi pears; they are crisper and sweeter than European pears. *Illustrated overleaf.*

2 Japanese pears, peeled and sliced
4 fresh or dried jujubes or dates
300ml/10fl oz/1¼ cups water
squeeze of lime juice
ice cubes, to serve

Place the pear slices and jujubes in a saucepan with the water and boil for 10 minutes. Once the fruit has softened, lightly mash it to release the juices. Pour the liquid through a sieve and discard the pulp. Squeeze a few drops of lime juice into the liquid and serve in glasses, over ice.

MANGO MILK

MANG GUO NIU NAI 芒果牛奶

SERVES 4

PREP TIME
5 MINUTES

Mango has a creamy consistency and combines particularly well with milk, for example in desserts like Mango Pudding (page 150). This non-alcoholic cocktail is a Chinese-inspired milkshake.

1 ripe mango, peeled and chopped
100g/3½oz/½ cup mango pulp
50ml/2fl oz/3 tbsp condensed milk
50ml/2fl oz/3 tbsp cold water
50ml/2fl oz/3 tbsp milk

Put all the ingredients into a blender and blend until thoroughly mixed. Pour into a glass and enjoy.

COLA GINGER (FOR COLDS AND FLU)

KE LE JIANG 可乐姜

SERVES 1

COOK TIME
5 MINUTES

'Achoo.' I could not stop sneezing and shivering, even though Guangzhou was scorching hot.

'Oh no, you're coming down with something,' observed my grandmother.

She marched me to a stand selling tonics, and asked for a cola ginger. I made a face. I hated that stuff, but I was determined not to be ill so I held my nose and downed the entire ceramic bowl. My grandmother nodded in unison with the shopkeeper, 'You'll be right as rain.'

The shopkeeper smiled and said, 'We Chinese have been drinking this stuff since the 13th century and look how strong we are! Ginger has healing qualities and it will fight your cold like a kung fu panda!'

We all laughed. I could imagine the ginger taking form to fight my mucus-lined lungs, sore throat and cough.

My grandmother added, 'And hopefully it will keep you calm. Stop being so anxious all the time. We're supposed to be on holiday.'

I smiled, but this time I was cringing as she talked about me in front of the shopkeeper. It was a good job I had lost my voice. I let them both give me their ten pennies' worth of opinions and closed my eyes. I felt like a ten-year-old child again, having my hand held by my grandmother every time I drank this stuff. Now that she's gone, I realize she was absolutely right and I make it to ward off colds and flu.

1 can of cola
1 thumb-sized piece of fresh root ginger, cut into thin slices

Heat the cola in a saucepan until boiling. Add the ginger and boil over a high heat for 3 minutes. Drink hot.

INDEX

First published in the United Kingdom in 2016 by Pavilion
1 Gower Street, London WC1E 6HD

ISBN: 978-1-91090-460-2

A CIP catalogue record for this book
is available from the British Library.

10 9 8 7 6 5 4 3 2 1

Reproduction by Mission, Hong Kong
Printed and bound by 1010 Printing International, China

This book can be ordered direct
from the publisher at:
www.pavilionbooks.com

Publisher's Acknowledgements
Commissioning editor: Emily Preece-Morrison
Recipe Photographer: Clare Winfield
Location Photography: see credits
Cover illustrator: Eri Griffin
Design direction: Laura Russell
Designer: Sophie Yamamoto
Home economist: Valerie Berry
Prop stylist: Wei Tang
Copy editor: Maggie Ramsay

Location Image Credits
6, 7, 9R, 10, 22, 60R, 61, 88, 89, 102,
128C, 129, 174C: Karen Thomas
8L, 9L, 128L and R: Clare Winfield
4: © Hemis / Alamy Stock Photo
8C: © Alex Segre / Alamy Stock Photo
8R: © Yadid Levy / Alamy Stock Photo
11: © Reimar 8 / Alamy Stock Photo
60L: © Alex Segre / Alamy Stock Photo
71: © Jack Young - Places / Alamy Stock Photo
113: © Design Pics Inc / Alamy Stock Photo
174L: © Alison Thompson / Alamy Stock Photo
175: © Lee MFL / Alamy Stock Photo

Thank you to Emily and the team at Pavilion, and our agent, Anne Kibel, for making this book a dream come true – it has been an amazing experience and a lot of fun! Thank you to Ken Hom, Alan Yau, Mitch Tonks and Matt Preston for your generous supporting quotes and inspiration.

This book is dedicated to God and our dear family: Mum, Dad, Janet and Peter, Jimmy, Katherine and Sam. We also dedicate this book to all our dear clients, including the Armitage and Chumate family, Alan, Adele and the Pearlman family, Anne, David and the Wilson family, Mr Simon Brown and the Fit Fam from 'The Class Is The Bomb', Animesh Gohil, Paul Wan, Derek and Angela Perrin, Jamie Bebb, Wai-Lam and Karen, Colin and Debra Hayward, Pastor Kim and MCCC, King's Church, Audacious Church and everyone who follows us on Twitter (@sweetmandarins), Facebook (Sweet Mandarin) and on Instagram (sweet.mandarin).

www.sweetmandarin.com

Alan Yau,
BBC broadcaster and food writer
'This really is a scrumptious book. Lisa and Helen have travelled across China in search of amazing street food and their selection of dishes shows the incredible range that's out there. Most importantly, the recipes are truly accessible – easy for anyone to make in the comfort of their own kitchen.'

Matt Preston,
food journalist, restaurant critic and writer
"Lisa and Helen put the 'yum' into yum cha. There's no one I'd rather pleat dumplings with than the Sweet Mandarin sisters."

Mitch Tonks,
restauranteur and food writer
"I've always been a big fan of street food and this brilliant book brings you right to the heart of it. If you want to reveal the mystery of real Chinese cooking, this is the book."